LIVING CAMEOS

Other books by Helen Hosier

Struck By Lightning, Then By Love
  (with Wilma Stanchfield)

Better Than I Was
  (with Frances Kelly)

The Other Side of Divorce

Jesus: Love in Action

It Feels Good to Forgive

LIVING CAMEOS

Helen Kooiman Hosier

Fleming H. Revell Company
Old Tappan, New Jersey

Unless otherwise identified, Scripture quotations in this book are taken from the King James Version of the Bible.

Scripture verses marked TLB are taken from *The Living Bible,* Copyright © 1971 by Tyndale House Publishers, Wheaton, Ill. Used by permission.

Library of Congress Cataloging in Publication Data

Hosier, Helen Kooiman.
    Living cameos.

    1. Christian biography—United States. 2. Women—
United States—Biography. I. Title.
BR1713.H64   1984   280′.092′2   84–3332
ISBN 0–8007–1398–2

TO
Peggy Fels

a choice gem, the dearest of friends, a Proverbs 31 woman if ever
I've met one, a precious soul whose memory I will cherish forever.

While writing this book, the thought occurred to me that I should
dedicate it to my good friend, Peggy Fels. But I decided to keep it
a secret. Yes, it would be a lovely surprise for her. In my first book
of *Cameos,* the dedication was to my mother, and Peggy had told
me on several occasions that the dedication touched her deeply and
that every time she read it, she cried. You see, I kept it a secret from
my mother, too, for my mother went to be with the Lord before the
book was published. The dedication then became a letter to my
mother, telling her that she was the dearest Cameo of all.

I could not know, of course, that on December 20, 1983, God
would take Peggy Fels to be with Himself. How I wept when the
call came! This explanation will help you to understand, I trust, the
words that follow.

Dearest Peggy,

You would have laughed and objected if I had told you that the
book was dedicated to you. You, like my precious mother,
would have reminded me that you had never attained any
greatness. But oh, my friend, you just never realized the full
impact you had on so many lives. I think you represent the
many women whose stories will never be told within the pages
of a book—women who are gentle and gracious, modest and
unassuming, loyal, kind, and always so supportive of others.

Peggy, you were such an inspiration to your husband, chil-

dren, and grandchildren, to your church family as a devoted
pastor's wife, and to your many friends. You were so incredibly
patient, and so magnificently kind. At your memorial service,
Pastor Joe quoted your husband as saying, "If I could think of
something Peggy had done wrong, it would be easier." And I
think that's how everyone felt. Your faith, the witness of your
life—you were exemplary, a lady very precious to our hearts.

The last time we were with you and Fred, he took me aside
and whispered, "Do you know Peggy prays for you by name
every day?" I knew you were a praying woman, Peggy, but that
really got to me. I shed some tears on the way home and said
to my husband, "I don't deserve that." You touched my life,
dear friend, and because of you, I have grown.

Peggy, my precious friend, how I loved you!

I want readers of this book to know something about you that
always caused me to marvel. You and Fred were married forty
years, and during that time, as a pastor's wife, you took into
your home thirty-eight people who desperately needed help. In
addition, you raised three beautiful children of your own. Your
hearts were so big—you were ready to embrace the entire needy
world, and so you reached out to your immediate world, giving
these individuals a place to live as long as they needed it and
providing for their every need. Peggy, I am almost certain that
when you reached heaven, among the first words you heard
were these: "Come, ye blessed of my Father, inherit the kingdom prepared for you from the foundation of the world: For
I was an hungred, and ye gave me meat: I was thirsty, and ye
gave me drink: I was a stranger, and ye took me in: Naked, and
ye clothed me: I was sick, and ye visited me: I was in prison,
and ye came unto me.

"Then shall the righteous answer him, saying, Lord, when
saw we thee an hungred, and fed thee? or thirsty, and gave thee
drink? When saw we thee a stranger, and took thee in? or
naked, and clothed thee? Or when saw we thee sick, or in
prison, and came unto thee?

"And the King shall answer and say unto them [unto you,
Peggy], Verily I say unto you [Peggy], Inasmuch as ye have

done it unto one of the least of these my brethren, ye have done it unto me" (Matthew 25:34–40).

Peggy, I have to agree with the pastor who ministered to all of us at your memorial service, your homegoing seems too early. But one of your sons explained it this way: "How God must have delighted in Mom all these years. It must have been difficult for Him not to take her home sooner."

And I have to remind myself, just as I would remind readers of this book, that our timetable isn't always the same as God's timetable. I think if you could talk to us now, you would say that too. I think also that you would tell us to live as though we were going to live forever, but be ready to go at any time.

I thank God for the beauty of your life, the example you left of godly living and Christlike loving, and the assurance we all had that you were rejoicing with the heavenly hosts at the feet of Jesus for your first Christmas in heaven. And oh, Peggy, whenever you see my mother in heaven, tell her for me, will you, that I think you are both precious Cameos and I miss each of you very much.

Your loving friend,

Helen

Dedicated also to
seven other very special
"Cameos"
who have come into my life in
recent years.
My life has been immeasurably blessed and enriched
because of your love and friendship.
Fern Lindquist
Nancy Vanderhider
Goldya Mills
Hortense Medlin
Iola Watkins
Carol Tate
Peggy Moore

Contents

Preface

In the still air the music lies unheard;
In the rough marble beauty hides unseen;
To make the music and the beauty needs
The master's touch, the sculptor's chisel keen.
Great Master, touch us with Thy skillful hands;
Let not the music that is in us die!
Great Sculptor, hew and polish us; nor let
Hidden and lost, Thy form within us lie!

These words by an unknown poet have etched themselves into my thinking. In particular, as I have worked on these cameo stories and thought about and observed the way in which the Great Sculptor has hewn and polished these "gems," a truth long ago discovered has crossed my thinking many times—chipping, carving, and sculpting are all necessary by a craftsman if a gem is to emerge a thing of beauty.

How much we would like to avoid the "chisel keen"! Oh, I know, for I have talked to you—you, who are also precious Cameos. And I know myself—there have been so many times when I have protested and begged to have relief from the hewing and the polishing.

So as I have written this, I have been talking to myself as much as to you—reminding us that the Great Master Sculptor knows what He is doing. I do love the way the Apostle Peter put it: ". . . trust yourself to the God who made you, for he will never fail you" (1 Peter 4:19 TLB).

I know that I have been accorded a rare privilege in spending time with the Cameos in this book. I am deeply indebted to them and their families; in addition, I appreciated the insights afforded by their associates in business and some of the ministries represented in these stories. These Cameos are such lovely, down-to-earth people. You would have enjoyed their homes and the hospitality they so graciously extended; that isn't possible, of course, and that's why they have so lovingly extended themselves to you in this way. Each of them, in one way or another, has commented that she wanted to be included only if I felt her story could genuinely help someone else and be a source of inspiration and blessing.

In the first book of cameo stories, I expressed the belief that God, in His goodness, gives all kinds of experiences to all kinds of women, and that we can learn and be helped by what God has done in others. That has been the purpose of this book—to show God's hand at work fashioning the lives of some of His children.

For years, wherever I have gone, women have expressed gratitude for the book *Cameos: Women Fashioned by God,* and in the next breath asked, "When are you going to do another *Cameos?*" During the summer of 1982 I was asked that question three times in one week. I am grateful for a conversation I had with Kathy Salerno (one of the Cameos in this volume), the third person who confronted me that memorable week, and her wise counsel suggesting that I seek God's will about compiling another such book of "living Cameos."

I not only did what Kathy suggested, I also did the near-at-hand thing—I met with the editors of the Fleming H. Revell Company. This book is the result. I am especially indebted to editor Fritz Ridenour for his unfailing good judgment, and for cheering me along as I felt some sculpting by the Master Sculptor even as this book was in process.

My gratitude extends to Martha Lloyd for a beautiful job of typescript, and to the Cameos at our Sunnyvale church for showing love and concern in so many thoughtful ways. Thanks also to family and friends, far and near, who prayed me through.

Finally, I thank you—the reader—unknown to me, but known to God. You, too, have a story to tell. Your story may never be written and published, but these words express it so well:

Life is like a book in volumes three,
  the past,
  the present,
  and the yet to be.
The first is done and laid away,
  the second we are writing every day.
But the third, and last, of the volumes three
  is locked from sight—
  God keeps the key.

I'm so glad He keeps the key, aren't you? I'm so thankful He can be trusted to help us write our life stories, and that we can recognize His touch and respond to it, knowing He will never fail us. Each of us chooses the way our life story is written, and what is written remains a record in God's *Book of Life.* To you, I would say,

Let His love forgive your past,

Let His peace take over your present,

and

Let His will be your will, for now and on into the unknown future. God is fashioning lovely, eternal Cameos. You are one of them. As one Cameo to another, may I encourage you to trust God to make you a precious jewel reflecting His glory.

Helen Hosier
Sunnyvale, California
December 1983

LIVING CAMEOS

I

Mary C. Crowley
The Woman Who Brags on God

"It is wonderful to be in the family of God. From my heavenly Father I have a sense of belonging. From my union with Jesus Christ I have a sense of worth, not worthy, but of greatest worth. And from the Holy Spirit, I have a sense of competency, of 'Can do.' "

He came behind her where she was sitting at the breakfast-room table, leaned over, and planted a kiss on her cheek. "Hmm, hmm, gorgeous," he said, as he walked away.

Mary Crowley looked up tenderly—basking, womanlike, in that brief exchange of affection—and gently patted his hand resting on her shoulder. "He really believes that. He feels that way," she said, laughingly adding, "There are lots more gorgeous women." She turned and watched as he left the room. There was a precious look of deep caring on her lovely face, and her eyes registered the security a loved woman feels as she explained, "We went together seven years before we could be married, and now we've been married thirty-five years."

What Mary Crowley was really saying was that she respected her husband, something she feels is basic to a good marriage.

"Marriage is a 150 percent proposition," she states. "You can't

bring just half of yourself to *any* relationship, but especially marriage.
You have to give your *total* self, and I think women have to bring
more to a relationship than men. But I think we are capable of it. I
think we have to be more adjustable—more flexible, that's what I'm
talking about. Yes, we have to go more than halfway, we have to
sometimes go a long way." She paused, reflecting, and I knew this
woman who has spent much of her lifetime working with and helping
other women was thinking about some of those women who have
shared their lives with her, and about her own long pilgrimage.

Four Hundred Million and Still Growing

Mary's pilgrimage has brought her to the position she holds today
—president and founder of Home Interiors and Gifts, Inc. Mary is
the brains and heart behind this Dallas-based, direct-sales company
that began with an initial investment of $5,000 in December 1957,
and spiraled to gross sales of more than $400 million in 1982.
Moreover, the business that Mary began as a one-woman operation,
shipping wares out of her garage, now encompasses every state in the
union, with a sales force of more than thirty-nine thousand associates
whom she calls "displayers." Six distribution centers in the Dallas
metroplex employ more than two hundred people in the office structure, and six hundred more in the distribution centers themselves,
with yet another eight hundred managers in the field—and it's
always growing.

"Phenomenal, isn't it?" Mary asks with a touch of awe in her
voice that lets you know *she* knows the accomplishment is not just
the result of self-effort. She's worked very hard, and so has everyone
else, but it's more than dedicated effort.

"Begin with a dream," she shared with her displayers and managers from the outset. "See yourself as an achiever, a queen. Reject the
idea that you're handicapped in any way. Imagine yourself as a
co-worker with God." Mary told them there was a form of "magic
in belief." She urged them to expect that great things were going
to happen, and then to work to bring them about. "It is not enough
to want. You must want *to*—you must want to *do* and to *be* somebody. Ten two-letter words can change your life: *If it is to be, it is
up to me.*"

Nothing to Brag on Except God

Mary visited Scotland with an evangelist a few years ago, and after she left one of the men said, "That woman goes around bragging on God. Over here we don't brag on Him, we complain to Him."

When she heard the comment, Mary responded, "Isn't it the truth? We have nothing to brag on except God." Mary credits God with the success of her enterprise.

"You can be anything you make up your mind to be," she says firmly. "You cannot help what you are now, but you *can* help what you will be tomorrow. God is able to make every one of us bigger and better.

"At Home Interiors we believe in giving God the glory, knowing that it is not because *we* are so terrific that we are prosperous, but that our success is God's gift, and without His help we would have nothing. The Lord's blessing is our greatest wealth."

Making Your Marriage Work While *You* Work

The code of ethics of Mary's business stresses that no home in America needs to be dull and unattractive. "Decor can make a difference—it can help show a woman's love for her family. The wife has to make her home a place where husband and children are drawn. She is the magnet. Wives must make their husbands see themselves as special—and working wives must make a special effort. Next to her relationship with God, the most wonderful relationship is the one in the home.

"The dearest thing to me is that every morning my husband tells me he loves me. The thing that makes marriage work is commitment —and not emotion."

The scene that opened this chapter was not just for your enjoyment; it was the result of the absolute basic way Mary sees marriage. "If your desire is to enrich your marriage, then you will make the effort. The chances are very likely that you will reap exactly what you sow. Make a goal of the commitment of your will and your mind to strengthening your marriage and you will be happy to find that your heart and your emotions will fall right in line."

She has always urged her managers and displayers, who work out of their homes, to arrange their work to accommodate the needs of their families. Displayers take their wares into the homes of hostesses who have invited guests for a Home Interiors party. One of the more attractive features of this work is the fact that a woman doesn't have to punch a time clock away from home—she is an independent contractor who sets her own hours. She doesn't have to neglect her family since parties can be scheduled at night when husbands are home to care for the children, or moms with school-age children can have morning get-togethers. "We thought of flex time long before the government did," Mary quips.

Life Taught Her Not to Take Anything for Granted

Busy as she has always been, Mary has worked at her marriage to Dave Crowley. Her first marriage in 1932 ended in desertion and eventual divorce. There were other, earlier, tragedies—the death of her mother when Mary was only eighteen months old, living with her beloved grandparents until she was not quite seven, then being cruelly wrenched away from them to live with her father and an uncaring stepmother in the state of Washington until she was thirteen, lonely years in high school, the teenage marriage that failed, the difficult years as a single when she wore the dual hats of breadwinner and mother, and a bout with cancer just a year after launching her business.

Remarriage in 1948 to David M. Crowley, Jr., brought into Mary's life the missing dimension that she, as a loving, caring woman longed for. "Working as closely as I have with women, I've learned that many wives don't know how to give their husbands happiness," she says. Out of that observation and her own experience grew a personal concern that has become an important dimension to her in counseling the many women who are a part of her business. Our experiences can make us bitter or better; Mary chose to allow them to make her better, to mold her into the woman she is today—a woman with an unbudgeable faith in God and unwavering confidence in herself.

Her grandparents had taught her that God was a personal God who cared about the affairs of His people, and that Jesus was her personal Friend and He loved her. When she was thirteen she made a commitment to Him and asked Him to be her personal Savior. As a result of her early childhood, Mary doesn't take anything for granted and has never lost her appreciation for the smallest kindness and comfort. "I pray daily that I will not let the day pass without helping someone else—if only to repay those who have helped me," she says.

Mary Wears Her House Well

One of the things she especially enjoys doing is sharing their home, Chapel Knoll, with others. It's a fifty-year-old, English-style home, furnished and accessorized in such a way as to reflect the gracious woman she is. "We wear our houses, as it were," she says, "and they need to look good on us." Mary's house is a lot like its owner—bright, cheerful, a genuinely delightful, unpretentious home. It is comfortable—from the spacious atrium to the pleasantly cluttered bookshelves in the family room, on into the adjoining country kitchen. The colors are restful, pleasing to the senses—from the tangerine-sherbet-colored carpet to the miscellany on walls, tables, and bookshelves. No wonder Mary's sales reps by the busload enjoy coming to see her every year. Mary wears her house well.

"The home should be a haven—a place of refuge, a place of peace, a place of harmony, a place of beauty. The home is one of the greatest influences on the character of mankind," she is fond of stating. Long before she began her now-famous business, these were principles Mary put into practice in her own home with her own two growing children. But once her business became established, these same principles became a part of her code of ethics, to which her associates and displayers subscribe.

God Doesn't Take Time to Make Nobodies

"Working with literally thousands of women I have found that their number one problem is lack of self-confidence," says Mary. "My own self-confidence is tied up in the character of God, so I know I don't have to worry about it. But it came as something of a surprise to me when I discovered that not all women—even Christian women—realize this. Maybe they know this to be true in their heads, but they don't feel it in their hearts. So one of the things we try to do is help women realize that they are created in God's image, and that they are designed to be special."

Because she believes that within most women there is genius potential, she says, "I'm dedicated to bringing out the genius in every one of them."

When Mary speaks about being glad she's a woman, her countenance really lights up. Someone described her smile as being as bright as polished sunshine. Her enthusiasm is catching and her version of creation makes women feel good about themselves. "When the Lord created the world, He looked at it and said, 'That's good.' Then He created man, looked at him, and said, 'That's good, but I believe I can do better.' So He created woman."

Her sparkling dark eyes twinkle and her nose crinkles when she laughingly tells that. There is something about Mary C. Crowley that speaks aliveness, excitement, contagious enthusiasm, and, yes, fun. Mary enjoys life; she is zestful, spirited.

She believes also in the worth of men, don't misunderstand, but she will quickly explain, "God knows who you are. He knows you by *your* name, not your husband's name. Women must understand that they are persons of great potential. One of the best things about being women is that we don't have to go out into the world and prove we're men! I speak from a full cup—I'm deeply glad I'm a woman."

Mary is big on goal setting. She points to Proverbs 16:9. "We should make plans—counting on God to direct us. There is little to be gained by falling into the trap of trying to achieve goals by wishing something would happen. That's just dreaming."

She has had two primary goals for her business, which she passes on to others: "Honor God; and bless and serve people." She enjoys telling you that in most companies P & L means Profit & Loss. "In Home Interiors, that means 'People & Love.' "

She is known for saying, "Be somebody, God doesn't take time to make a nobody." Mary believes in providing the backup support that the women in her company need in order to reach their fullest potential. "I say to them, 'I want you to realize who you are, and be glad about it. Then you can look at others for what they are and not be in competition with them.' Our self-esteem must not come to us from happenings or from what other people say about us. So often it does, and then when somebody says something that makes us feel bad, down goes our self-esteem. If they brag on us, it goes up. That is a barometer we can't afford, because then we can be devastated by someone's remarks. Of course we want to please people and have friends, but our self-esteem must come, first of all, from our relationship with God Himself."

Aspiration + Inspiration + Perspiration = Success

Mary's own career began when, as a single parent with no particular marketable skills and two children to support, she had to join CPAs, teachers, and bank presidents who were walking the streets looking for jobs. It was the time of the Great Depression. Mary remembered one of her grandmother's wise sayings. "She had taught me that when things happen to you, you can lose only if you react to them rather than using the experience to progress." Mary chose to progress.

With a calm sense of self-assurance that was to characterize her personality, she went out and landed a sales position. As a result of this, she was hooked on selling as a career. And she was determined to succeed.

In the following years she bettered herself with other jobs, moving up the pay scale after taking a series of night classes in accounting. Then she worked for an insurance company, and still later in the furniture business. She was introduced to the home party plan through selling Stanley Home Products, and then worked as sales manager for an import company. But it took a personally traumatic time in her life at this juncture to bring her own business into being.

Her strong Christian beliefs and her business methods based on scriptural principles came into conflict with the owners of the company and in November 1957 she found herself out of a job. It was a jolt. It was also one time in her life when she threw herself down on the sofa and started to cry—but only briefly. She was about to work herself into a case of the self-pities when a vision of her grandmother, standing in her long, white apron flashed into her mind. "Don't live in 'if only' land, Mary."

She got up, dried her tears, bathed, and, dressed in her nicest outfit, went to see her friend Ralph Baker. When Mary had first moved her little family to Dallas, they joined the First Baptist Church, where Dr. George W. Truett was the pastor. It was there that Ralph and his wife befriended Mary and her children, Don and Ruthie. Ralph and Dr. Truett had helped her see that the will of God is always right and safe. Now she was remembering their counsel.

"Any experience we go through, from a broken heart to a mistake in handling our children, can be used by God to help us realize His love. To help me remember that the will of God is safe, I put a sign over my mirror that read: JESUS NEVER FAILS but also JESUS NEVER FAILS ME."

Ralph Baker encouraged Mary and lined up a new job for her, but Mary hesitated. For a long time a lot of the women with whom she worked had been urging her to set up her own direct-sales company. "I knew that was what I really wanted to do. If I had my own company, I could set the standards I wanted upheld, and I could be as generous as I wanted with the commissions. What would happen if I started a business that was really dedicated to helping women create happier homes? Wouldn't it just have to succeed? Nobody knew me and I didn't have the capital or the contacts with suppliers. Or so I thought. . . .

"God saved me from the deadly, crippling diseases of self-pity and resentment," she says today. "He gave me courage and determination to start all over again. The result was that I went into business for myself, and Home Interiors and Gifts came into being. Out of this I learned that when God opens doors, you get up and go through them."

When Dave Crowley came home from work that night, instead of the red-eyed wife he'd left in the morning, he found a bubbling Mary, wide-eyed and excited over the day's events. Quickly she unfolded the plan for her dream of having her own business, then, pausing, she looked at him and said, "There's just one thing, Dave."

"What's that?" he asked.

"I'll have to work hard. . . . If you don't want me to do this, just say so and I won't."

"Honey," Dave responded, "if you don't go into business, the world of business will be the loser."

Today she adds, "I had my husband's approval, my suppliers, and the outlines for a brand-new company. The day that had dawned with the funeral for my old career was ending with the birth of my very own company. Out of my disappointment came victory.

"This experience reinforced a lesson I had learned as a child while living with my father and stepmother: You never gain by sitting around feeling sorry for yourself. Attitude is the mind's paintbrush. It can color a situation gloomy and gray, or cheerful and gay. In fact, attitudes are more important than facts."

Ten days later, Home Interiors and Gifts, Inc., was official, with loans, charter, and details taken care of to make Mary's dream become a full-fledged reality. Success didn't come overnight, however, and in looking back Mary remembers her first year in business as a blur of eighty-hour workweeks. Succeeding years have never seen Mary resting on her laurels.

You Can't Outgive God

Despite her success, Mary has never tried to take all the credit. She realizes that God gave her the energy to put in eighty hours a week when she started out, and she's thankful He continues to give her strength for an unbelievable schedule. She is well aware that she needs to give back to God what He has given to her.

A fun-loving and generous person, Mary also takes delight in spreading the wealth around among those who earn it. Yearly seminars provide a time of recognizing achievements of the past year at an awards gala for the women.

As a young woman Mary learned to tithe and to give God a chance to provide for her needs and expectations. The Bible taught tithing—giving 10 percent of one's income back to the Lord. In those early days she was struggling to support two small children and it wasn't easy, but she emphatically tells you, "You can't outgive God. So if you want financial security—not necessarily abundance, but security—I urge people to honor the Lord with their substance (Proverbs 3:9, 10) and 'Prove the Lord if He will not open the windows of heaven, to pour you out a blessing so there will not be room enough to receive it' (*see* Malachi 3:10). But give for the joy of giving—if you only 'give to get' you are not giving, you are trading," she cautions.

She likes to refer to Matthew 6:21 where it says, "For where your treasure is, there will your heart be also." She asks, "If we can trust God with our salvation, can't we also trust Him with our finances?" Mary found Him to be totally trustworthy.

Mary Crowley has an ongoing working partnership with God. Her generosity overflows in many directions—from turning her employees loose with shopping carts in Safeway stores at Christmastime, to donating the chapel in the Medical City Dallas Hospital, to the Mary C. Building at the First Baptist Church of Dallas, to giving her support to youth homes, colleges, scholarships, the American Cancer Society, the Fellowship of Christian Athletes, and on and on it goes.

"God invented giving," she reminds you. "People need to give and share. Just one little boy's lunch was given to Jesus, and He fed a multitude. The obedience is ours and the miracle is His. It really isn't our money anyway, we're just stewards of it. I couldn't enjoy amassing money and seeing other people have needs and not do something about it. And it gives joy, and it helps others."

She usually wears a necklace holding two silver shovels of different sizes. Asked to explain the symbolism, she says, "A young man from South Africa—one of several I've been able to help through school —gave it to me along with this story: A philanthropist was asked how he could give away so much and have so much left over. He answered, 'I guess it's like this, I shovel it out and God shovels it in, and He's got a bigger shovel.' " This is one of her favorite stories; but it is also a fitting tribute to the wearer.

Mary's giving is not just financial. Her friend, Edith Schaeffer, speaks of Mary's greater giving in the form of time, talents, energy, thought, prayer, emotion, love, and communication—not only with groups but also with compassion on a person-to-person basis. This was demonstrated as Mary and I were speaking about the busyness of just living and scheduling one's time. "This Thursday night I'm speaking up at a little church in a nearby community. It's the church of one of our employees. They asked me to come a long time ago and I put it on my calendar. You have to ask yourself, *Does God want me to do this?*" she explained.

"For our employees I try to do the things that will help them. If you'd look at my calendar you'd be inclined to say, 'Mary, you don't have time to go,' but you see, I've made a commitment and I'm going to keep it. A promise is a promise." Mary is a woman of *integrity*—a beautiful word to describe an attribute that is not always so plentiful in the world today.

Her Guidelines for Living

Early in her dual role as breadwinner and mother, Mary set down some guidelines to help in basic decision-making to avoid being overwhelmed. Psalm 37 provided the framework. "That Psalm doesn't say you can escape responsibilities. Victory comes from managing life, facing it head-on." Here are her guidelines:

1. *Choose to do the essentials from among the things you want and must do.* Essentials are (a) learning to develop your character in God's image, (b) faithfulness in your family life, (c) absolute honesty on the job, and (d) helping those who need you.

2. *Rid your life of anxiety.* Worry never robs tomorrow of its sorrow; it only saps today of its strength. When Mary felt herself falling into the trap of self-pity, she learned to get up and do something constructive immediately. If she felt tired, she gained energy by telling herself that she felt great. If she dreaded an especially worrisome task, she chose to do it first and get it out of the way. Getting rid of anxiety also means not harboring ill will against anyone (Matthew 18:21, 22).

3. *Delight in the Lord.* Learn to praise Him daily. After she learned to delight herself in the Lord, and to trust Him to solve her problems, she could simply say, "Okay, Lord, it's Your show. This is up to You."

Among her practical guidelines for living life to the fullest is her frequent admonition to "learn to forgive and forget." She emphasizes, "Our heavenly Father is our example."

She then illustrates, "Marriage, for instance, demands a lot of give-and-take, and we must be sure that we are not taking more than we are giving. We need to be sensitive to what is needed in *all* our relationships with others, and then we need to learn how to give it graciously, from the heart. Sometimes we just need to give in, although we know that we are in the right and the other person should be the one to give in. Who cares? Give in anyway. Remember that it is possible to win the battle and still lose the war. That's not so smart. We need to learn to be good givers—and good forgivers!"

Mary's "Can Do" Philosophy

More than anything, Mary likes to brag on God. "When I realized one day what it cost Him to redeem me, then I fully realized my worth. I try to help other women, in particular, see this," she modestly explains.

"In this age of what I call 'distractomania,' there are so many things horning in to distract each of us. These *things* distract us from our chief aim in life. God created us to have fellowship with Him. That is basic. He created us to live in this world with a social nature so we can have relationships with others that are satisfactory, but I do not believe any relationship can be satisfactory for very long unless the relationship with God the Father is intact. I think that is so vital. So many women do not feel that wonderful confidence in Him and, therefore, in themselves.

"I am so grateful He gave me that. I have never felt like there was anything I couldn't do."

Many years ago she read the story of Deborah in the Old Testament (Judges 4), and thought to herself: *"I just wonder what God could do with Mary Crowley."* Then she said aloud, "I want to give Him a chance."

As I prepared to leave Mary's house, she said, "Oh, you must see our chapel," and she called for her husband. Dave escorted us down a crushed marble pathway and across an arched bridge over a spring-fed creek, cutting through the back lawns of their wooded acreage. There, on a little knoll, I saw a lovely, rustic, outdoor chapel.

Dave talked as we walked. "Mary grew up loving an old hymn called 'The Church in the Wildwood.' Well, when we moved here she said, 'Oh, Dave, now we have enough space. Let's have a chapel of our own.' It's given her a lot of satisfaction and joy."

We stepped inside the little chapel. Light streamed in through stained-glass windows. My attention was immediately drawn to the wall. "Mary's favorite Scripture," he explained.

There, in Old English script, I read: "Thus saith the Lord, Let not the wise man glory in his wisdom, neither let the mighty man glory in his might, let not the rich man glory in his riches: But let him that glorieth glory in this, that he understandeth and knoweth me, that I am the Lord which exercise lovingkindness, judgment, and righteousness, in the earth: for in these things I delight, saith the Lord" (Jeremiah 9:23, 24).

These are fitting words. Fitting words that sound like Mary Crowley, the woman who brags on God. She doesn't glory in riches or sales of $400 million a year. She glories in the wisdom that God has given her. She glories in understanding and knowing the Lord. Indeed, she is a woman who brags on God.

Books by Mary C. Crowley: *Women Who Win, A Pocketful of Hope,* and *You Can Too,* all published by the Fleming H. Revell Company.

2

Shirley Dobson

From Shaky Childhood to Secure Womanhood

"For a long time everyone thought I had my life all together; no one knew I struggled with feelings of low self-esteem related to my difficult childhood. . . ."

The day I met her, Shirley Dobson was wearing a bright green shirtwaist dress that set off her blondish brown hair. "Summer colors," she laughed. "A lot of women are having themselves color-analyzed. I've had it done; it helps to make you feel good about yourself when you know the colors are right for you. It's important to develop a good self-image. For a long time everyone thought I had my life all together; no one knew I struggled with feelings of low self-esteem related to my difficult childhood. Only Jim understood it."

Low self-esteem—it's a problem many people struggle with and it might surprise us to know just who those individuals are. As Shirley said, very few people knew this was *her* problem until the day came when she was willing to admit it publicly.

"When a person has experienced traumatic family problems in the early years," Shirley says, "your great desire is to conceal the details from those around you. That's what I did until several years after I was married. I was so embarrassed by my childhood that I told no one about it except my husband. Because of that concealment, the pain of those early experiences remained very much alive within me. Then one day, Jim spontaneously asked me to share my testimony in his adult Sunday school class. He wanted me to relate what God had done for me, which meant opening those old wounds which I had carefully buried!"

Shirley's initial reaction was to resist her husband's invitation. Dr. Dobson then asked her to pray about the matter and give him an answer that Saturday.

"The more I prayed about the possibility of revealing my past, the more God seemed to put His thumb in my back. I *knew* He wanted me to do it. It was as though He were saying, 'I want you to share what I've done for you as an encouragement to those who have also gone through traumatic childhoods.' Reluctantly, I told Jim I would accept his request.

"The following Sunday morning, I spoke to 135 young married couples about my early home life and the problems I had experienced. It was one of the most difficult things I've ever done, but God blessed my obedience. Many people were crying by the time I had finished."

In her devotions a few days later, Shirley said to the Lord, "If You want me to tell this story in other places and settings, I will do it."

Within a week, she was asked to speak at a mother-daughter banquet and she accepted. As Shirley continued to open these hidden portions of her past, a marvelous inner healing began to occur.

As she says, "Jim helped me see that God not only wanted to heal the deep wounds I carried, but also to use my experience in the lives of others. That is, in fact, why I'm sharing my story."

Your needs may be similar to or completely different from Shirley Dobson's, but such vulnerability and honesty before God and others does have cleansing virtue.

The Grass Wasn't Always So Green

The lawn in front of Shirley Dobson's colonial-style California home is a lovely shade of green, but she didn't always look out on green grass. In fact, at one point in her life there wasn't *any* grass. And if someone had said many years ago to a little girl named Shirley that the grass was *not* greener on the other side of the fence, she would have remained firmly unconvinced.

"We were living in a run-down house with holes in the wall where my drunken father had shoved his fists in anger. I was so embarrassed over the condition of our home that I wouldn't invite friends to spend the night. I knew their houses didn't have holes in the wall, and they did have green, grassy yards."

Shirley's mother was a loving woman who knew she needed all the help she could get to raise her daughter and son. That's why she sent them to a neighborhood church when they lived in Torrance, California. That's where Shirley's impressionable young mind began to grasp the truth about Jesus. "My Sunday school teacher told us that God loved all of us and He knew *each* of *our* names." For the little girl who felt like nobody, this was incredibly good news!

"The first memory verse this teacher taught me was, 'In my Father's house are many mansions: if it were not so, I would have told you. I go to prepare a place for you' (John 14:2).

"I was astounded to learn that Jesus was preparing a mansion that would be *mine* someday! I could just visualize not being embarrassed to have friends over. Gradually, I developed a personal relationship with Jesus and gave my heart to Him at an altar of prayer. For the first time in my life, I went to bed that night with the knowledge that my sins had been forgiven and I was loved as a child of God."

Unfortunately, Shirley's parents continued to have marital conflict, which ended in divorce after her father had been unfaithful. That's when this little girl began asking God for a special favor.

"I got on my knees and asked Him, first, to send a Christian father into our home. A year later, my mother met the man who was to become my stepdad. I loved him instantly, and he has been a wonderful father to my brother and me. This was such a fantastic confirmation to my young faith, as I realized that God really did hear and answer prayer!"

Shirley also made a second request of the Lord during those early years. She began praying that God would give her a Christian husband when the time came for her to get married. She asked for the kind of loving, stable home that she had not experienced up to that point in her childhood.

Seven years later, she graduated from high school and left home to attend Pasadena College, a four-year liberal arts college. She was very popular in school, eventually being elected Homecoming Queen, senior class president, a member of Who's Who in American Colleges and Universities, and so on. But the most important event during her college career occurred during her sophomore year. She met a six-foot-two, blond, former Texan named Jim Dobson. He was captain of the tennis team and already had big plans to become a psychologist. They had a whirlwind courtship through that year— filled with laughter and fun and a few fusses and fights to make it all the more interesting. Shirley saw a depth of character and a strong sense of values in Jim that was missing in some of the other men she had dated. He had an unshakable faith in God and knew just where he wanted to go in life. Perhaps that's why Shirley decided, before he, that they should spend their lives together.

Jim graduated from college at the end of that year and was required to serve a term in the army. On the eve of his departure, he shocked her by saying that he felt they should break up. While he had enjoyed their times together, he was not certain that he wanted to marry her. His concern was that she would remain true to him while he was gone, missing the opportunities to date other men in her senior year and failing to find someone else to love.

"His motive was very magnanimous, but I still felt as though he had ripped my heart out," she says. Jim had always been independent and secure in his relationship with Shirley, which was the challenge that made her admire him. But now, he intended to walk out of her life. Their future together hung in the balance on that distressing evening.

Nevertheless, Shirley kept her poise. She hid her feelings from Jim and professed to agree that they should break up. After all, she was an expert at concealing her inner pain—she had been doing that for a lifetime. Jim walked her to the door of the dormitory and asked if he could kiss her good-bye. She said, "No, I'd rather you wouldn't." They smiled awkwardly at one another and Shirley went inside.

"It all hit me when I got to my room," she says. "I fell across my bed and cried all night. The one I loved so dearly was gone. All that remained were memories of the times we had had together—of Jim's incredible sense of humor and the loving way he had treated me. That was the most painful night of my life."

What Shirley didn't know was that Jim was doing some thinking, too. As he drove to the army base the next day, he realized for the first time that he had lost his best friend. Within minutes after his arrival at Fort Ord, California, he sat down and wrote Shirley a four-page letter, telling her that he had made an enormous mistake and asking her to forgive him. Two hours later, he called to assure her of his love and commitment. A few months later, Shirley agreed to become Mrs. James Dobson. She's never regretted that decision.

A Ring on Her Finger

Jim gave Shirley a ring on Christmas Eve, after having hidden a tape recorder under a pile of presents around the tree. At the appropriate moment as the family prepared to open the gifts, a "voice" spoke from the base of the tree—confirming their love and announcing the approaching wedding date. Shirley's ring was in one of those small packages that were distributed on that happy evening.

"Jim and I went together for three years before we were married. That gave us plenty of time to get to know each other, which is related to the success of our relationship. We feel it is important for couples to become friends before they are lovers, and to make this important decision very cautiously and deliberately. Jim counsels with many couples who have rushed things and found themselves married before they were hardly acquainted.

"Today," she continues, "I tell our daughter, Danae, not to settle for anyone less loving or admirable than her dad. I know that's a high standard to set for her, but that's how I feel. She agrees."

A Working Woman

Does Shirley Dobson know what it means to be a working wife and mother? Yes, she does. "I taught school for five years before Danae was born. Then a year after her birth, we were struggling to pay Jim's final graduate school bills at the University of Southern

California, and we had very little furniture in the house. That's when I began substitute teaching in a local school district. Two years later when Jim took Danae to the nursery school one day, she clung to his neck and begged him not to leave her. That night, we talked about Danae's need for a full-time mother and I agreed to quit. I have not worked outside the home since then. And somehow, we met our financial obligations—at first by selling and 'eating' one of our two Volkswagens."

Because of this experience, Shirley is sympathetic about the pressures facing today's working mothers. "I know many women have no choice about whether or not to seek employment," she says. "The last thing I want to do is put a guilt trip on those who are doing what they have to do.

"On the other hand, I do feel it is important for couples to decide what their priorities are. We are living in a very materialistic society and we are continually confronted with false values being fed to us by the media. There is a tendency to place greater emphasis on things and possessions than on family values and togetherness."

Shirley and I talked about this—the bartering of golden hours—women trading the joys and satisfaction of being full-time mothers for a paycheck. "It's an individual matter, involving many different circumstances," she said. "Basically, each woman has to decide how she can best meet all the demands and obligations that are on her as a wife and mother. But whatever her conclusion, it is still important for mothers to be available when their children want and need them.

"Of course, we also have a responsibility to develop ourselves as persons even while we are busy wives and mothers. If a home-maker allows herself to bog down intellectually and isolates herself from people, or becomes addicted to TV soaps, or becomes bored, it doesn't matter how much her husband loves or respects her, she still will lack a sense of self-respect. Self-esteem is sometimes a matter of self-choice. While our environment may not always be conducive to elevating our spirits, we do have it within our power to accept our limitations and make the most of our resources with God's help."

Life in a Fishbowl

The Dobson household is different from other families in several ways. "We know that we live in a fishbowl," Shirley says. "I suppose some people expect our children to be perfect, but our son and daughter are very normal kids. They have their arguments and their times of irresponsibility like other children. But there's a great deal of love in our home, too, and we are very close to one another. We've tried to bring up our son and daughter according to the principles my husband speaks and writes about, with a balance between love and discipline.

"Our lives became very hectic after my husband's first book, *Dare to Discipline,* was published and became a best-seller. There was a time when he felt as if he was standing alone by endorsing biblical concepts of authority and speaking out for the need for more parental leadership. Instead of being criticized, however, Jim was immediately thrust into the Christian limelight. He received thousands of requests for speaking commitments, magazine articles, radio and television appearances, and so on. He handled all of this pretty well, although it made our home even more hectic.

"We reached a crisis in 1978. Jim was accepting speaking assignments at the rate of six days per month. He refused to exceed that limit because of the need to preserve our family life. However, even being gone that amount of time began to weigh on his mind. Danae was thirteen and Ryan eight at the time, and he wanted to be with them on weekends. Saturdays and Sundays were the days his services were most wanted in Minneapolis, Atlanta, and Seattle. After a time of prayer, he met with his agent and asked him to cancel all future speaking engagements, even though he was receiving a very lucrative fee at the time."

Five months later, Dr. Dobson held the last of the citywide meetings which could not be cancelled, and permitted Word Publishers to videotape the entire event. It became the Focus on the Family film series which has now been seen by 37 million people around the world. And while these films were being seen by people Dr. Dobson could never have reached personally, he was at home raising his children and being a husband to Shirley.

From that decision has come another means of communication. He now has a nonprofit ministry by the same name, Focus on the Family, which includes a thirty-minute daily radio program heard on 460 stations, as well as ministries based on books, tapes, and television. More than one hundred thirty employees are needed to help the Dobsons handle the forty-five thousand letters they receive per month. Shirley serves on the board of directors for this organization, and occasionally joins her husband in the broadcast studio to express her own ideas. "It is very exciting work," she says.

For relaxation, the Dobson family ski, play tennis and basketball, and enjoy music. They also enjoy reading. Shirley particularly enjoyed J.I. Packer's book *Knowing God.* As she said, "It is one thing to know *about* God, as in the same sense that I know about Abraham Lincoln or William Shakespeare. But it is something entirely different to know God, *Himself!* Packer's book helped me get better acquainted with the Lord as a personal Friend and Savior."

Shirley's Walk of Faith

Shirley has put the no-grass, holes-in-the-wall house of her childhood far behind her. "Our home is very traditional. I like the Williamsburg era, so it's done in summer colors—federal blue, yellow, and a touch of cranberry—all kind of country formal. We bought the house in 1972 when California prices were only 20 percent of their present value. We have no desire to move, today, even though we have no room for the frequent guests we would like to entertain. We would rather make an understatement than an overstatement with our home and life-style. We want people to see Jesus first in our life and not things, so we try to keep everything in perspective. I thank and praise the Lord for what He has allowed us to have, but I don't hold anything too tightly."

If you were to walk up the drive to the Dobson home, you might hear Shirley playing the piano. "It's a tremendous emotional release for me. I'm not great at it, but I love classical music. My mother gave me this appreciation for music by providing piano lessons, even when money was tight."

Shirley has also been one of the cofounders of the Arcadia Chris-

tian Celebrity Series in her hometown. It is an annual luncheon
provided for non-Christian women who are invited to hear a well-
known guest speaker. There, they are greeted by one of the thirty-
two hostesses and are invited to join a weekly Bible study class to
learn more about the Word. Shirley has taught one of these classes
for two years, seeing many women come to a personal relationship
with Jesus Christ.

Today, Shirley's outlook and value system are rooted in her Christian faith. "Healing and fulfillment come as you look beyond yourself," she says. "I am often reminded of 2 Corinthians 5:7 where we
are told that we are to walk by faith, not by sight. I know this is true.
It is the best way to be aware of who I really am—I'm a child of God.
I've been created by Him as a unique individual. God doesn't want
us to compare ourselves to others—to what they have or how they
look. He accepts us as we are! And the past need not limit the
present or the future. If we let Him, He will help us to forget the
painful memories and overcome the struggles of a difficult childhood. He certainly did that for me. And I will always be grateful that
He heard those two desperate prayers that I uttered as a child.
Everything good in my life today has resulted from His lovingkindness in that hour of need. I'm no longer ashamed to tell my
story."

Shirley Dobson and Gloria Gaither have co-authored a unique book for
Christian wives and mothers entitled *Let's Make a Memory*, with the
subtitle "How to give the family tree nourishing roots." It is an intriguing
and illuminating book that will stimulate your thinking as to how you can
nourish your own family roots and create memorable traditions that will
bind your family together long after time and distance separate all of you.

3

Mary Dorr

Born to Talk and to Conquer Adversity

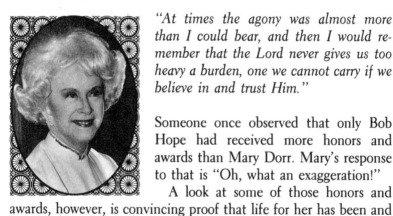

"At times the agony was almost more than I could bear, and then I would remember that the Lord never gives us too heavy a burden, one we cannot carry if we believe in and trust Him."

Someone once observed that only Bob Hope had received more honors and awards than Mary Dorr. Mary's response to that is "Oh, what an exaggeration!"

A look at some of those honors and awards, however, is convincing proof that life for her has been and is busy and fulfilling. Religious Heritage of America conferred on her its Faith and Freedom Award. Pepperdine University gave her its Distinguished Diploma of Merit, which it has bestowed only a few times in its long history. Golden State University conferred on her its Doctorate of Humanities. She is past national president of American Women in Radio and Television; and she traveled the world to organize the World Congress of Women in Radio and Television. The mother of four, she was voted California's Mother of the Year in 1977.

As former national public relations director of volunteer activities for the American Bible Society, she was in demand as a speaker throughout the nation. And since 1974 she has been the executive director of Religion in Media (RIM), a Hollywood-based, interfaith organization set up to improve the moral and spiritual content of films, television shows, books, record albums, and every form of the media. A tall, striking woman, she is perhaps best known from coast to coast through her weekly half-hour television interviews with celebrities and individuals from all walks of life.

Mary Dorr has been talking for years. "My mother always said I was 'born to talk.' I talked very early, imitating adults. My father was a powerful speaker. He had a bank in Megargel, Texas, where I was born, and for many years was a Texas state senator," she explains. "But my father was the master of the house, who felt that girls should be seen and not heard, and I had three sisters and one brother. So we weren't allowed to speak out very often at home. When my father wasn't around, I made up for lost time and I guess I've been doing it ever since! But I adored my father and even after I began public speaking in junior high school, he still said a woman's place was in the home and certainly not on the platform."

The Voice

While her father was strict and very traditional, and would probably even be called a chauvinist today, he was also a very dedicated Christian who made sure his family got to church and learned the Scriptures. The thing Mary remembers best from her childhood is going to church services morning and evening on Sundays, and to Wednesday night prayer meetings with her parents. "I learned early about the love of Jesus. I loved to read and the New Testament became my favorite Book. That love of reading stayed with me. I am never alone when I have the company of a good book.

"But I knew the Bible as well as my deacon father by the time I was eight. I could read a verse just once and have it memorized. I could hardly wait for Sundays to come so I could go to Sunday school and recite the verses I'd learned and receive a gold star. By the time I was sixteen, I knew many verses by memory and later, when my father died, and I was alone with him at the time, those verses helped me just as they would many times in the years ahead when I was faced with trauma and tragedy."

Mary's family moved to Long Beach, California, when she was a child. Her father lost everything in the Wall Street crash of 1929, then fell ill, and her mother had to support the family. She couldn't quite make it, so at eleven Mary was scrubbing floors, cleaning out toilets, and making beds for an apartment house.

"I'd get two hours of work in before I dashed off for school and then another three after school."

In high school she entered every debate and declamation contest and walked off with honors every time. She represented her school, speaking before civic clubs in southern California. As a result of this, she was already launched into radio at the age of fourteen. She heard that the California Chain Store Association was looking for "a voice" for an advertising campaign. She auditioned along with hundreds of applicants before a selection committee that chose her as the best.

"I earned a fortune for those days," she recalls. "Five dollars for every sixty-second spot I did."

"The Girl on the Street"

At sixteen she was graduated from Polytechnic High School, the valedictorian of her class. The next fall she begged a ride from a friend and arrived on the University of California campus at Berkeley with ten dollars in her purse. She wasn't bothered by the fact she had no job, the Great Depression was on and thousands roamed the streets looking for work.

"I guess I was too young to be scared," she says. "I rationed twenty-five cents a day for food, talked the university into letting me pay some of my fees later, bunked with a girl friend, and knocked on the doors of every radio station within miles."

An Oakland station, KWBR, hired her. "At that time," she says, "it was quite the vogue for men announcers to interview people on the street about some news event. Maybe I wasn't the first 'girl on the street' but I had to be among the first, and I drew a mob."

With that job and another one at a Berkeley station, KRE, she worked her way through the university and was started on a lifelong career that later took her to radio and television stations in Washington, D.C., where she covered the White House; Philadelphia, where she starred in a daily television show; San Francisco; and Hollywood. She married her university sweetheart, John Dorr, a young IBM salesman who was to become, during a thirty-year career, one of IBM's top executives.

A Working Wife and Mother

In the next several years four sons and one daughter were born, and the family moved about considerably. "We used to say that IBM meant 'I've Been Moved,'" she laughingly recalls. "Of course every time we moved there were tears from the children, but I think it was a wonderful learning experience for them. I would say to them, 'Whom do you believe in? Who is by your side every single minute?' and they knew that was God."

Mary wisely told her children, "Put a nice smile on your face and you will get a smile back, maybe not from everybody, but you will quickly make new friends that way." As a result of this kind of dialogue, Mary feels her children grew up to be very well-adjusted.

She managed to combine a career with being a wife and mother very effectively, but attributes much of this to the help she received from having a live-in widowed mother. Everywhere they lived, Mary worked. She broadcast for different radio stations all over the country, whether it was Salem, Oregon, or in White Plains, New York.

Her husband was an astute businessman and, in time, they owned their own seaplane, a flying yacht, which seated twenty-two people with all the gear fore and aft. There was a sunken galley in the middle. Actually, it was a flying home that could land equally well on water or the roughest terrain. They had flown to many vacation spots, sometimes over a thousand miles away; and they were outfitting the plane for a special sabbatical her husband was going to take. They were planning to fly around the world with their children.

"One of our favorite places was up in the wilds in British Columbia. Another time we flew into a wilderness area in Idaho, the Sawtooth Mountains, a place only planes could go, and they had to land in little meadows or on the rivers. While we were there, it occurred to me that this was such a primitive area and I got to thinking, who would lift us off the ground, who would get us out of there if something happened to my husband? I said to myself, *If a man can fly with skill, why not a woman?"*

That was the beginning for Mary of many months of hard study and effort. She came home to conquer flying, all the while keeping it a secret from her husband, taking lessons between her radio and TV shows. Finally, at Christmastime 1967, when John Dorr unwrapped his present from Mary it was to find his wife's license. "You have never seen such a shocked man in your life," she recalls. After that, whenever they were flying, her husband would give her the controls many times. And she acquired her own little plane, a Cherokee.

No Stranger to Tragedy

In August 1969 the Dorr family flew up to British Columbia for a camping outing. They'd had a wonderful time, but Mary had to get back to Hollywood to tape some shows. Her husband and twenty-year-old son, John, stayed behind to do some fishing with five American businessmen and their sons who flew in just as Mary and her other children were leaving.

"There were twelve of them all together. They were planning to enjoy each other's company, to fish, and just to relax away from phones and the business world. They didn't catch any fish all day Sunday and by Monday hadn't caught any either. So they decided to do some lake hopping. They went back about a mile across Lake Trembler for the taxi run up and then John gave it the gas, and just as he pulled back on the wheel, about six feet above the water, he fell forward dead over the wheel."

Mary's son was sitting in the copilot's seat and didn't know that his father had died instantly of a massive coronary, so he screamed, "Medic!"

"That's the ironic part," says Mary, "that I, who knew how to fly, wasn't there. No one on that plane knew how to fly!"

Several of the men pulled John Dorr out of the pilot's seat, and Johnny later moved into it. But for the time being, he stayed in the copilot's seat, knowing he somehow had to take control. The plane was lumbering ahead and Johnny was momentarily panic-stricken

because trees were coming right up at the water's edge. In describing
it later, he recalled that he looked up and there was this giant
mountain. He remembered reading somewhere that a plane will stall
if you pull back too fast. So he slowly pulled back on the wheel and
just dusted the tops of the trees and up over the mountaintop. He
figured out how to put it in a bank and they slowly circled the lake.

He said it suddenly occurred to him that he would have to try to
reach civilization. He was frightened, but he thought to himself,
What would Mom do if she were here? She would pray. So he calmed
right down and prayed, *Please God, I don't care about myself, but
I do care for Dad and want to get him to a hospital, and I care for
these five men and their five sons. Please help me, God.*

A still, small voice came into his mind—*Use the radio.*

He didn't even know what the radio looked like with dozens of
instruments above and all around him, but he figured it out and, with
the microphone in one hand while trying to maintain the wheel in
the other hand, he went up and down the dial saying, "We are an
American plane; we are somewhere in the wilderness area of British
Columbia—there are twelve men aboard with no pilot."

Suddenly, speakers came on and a Canadian Pacific airliner was
picking up his message. The pilot gave him instructions and told him
that in about an hour and a half he would see civilization down below
at a little place called Prince George which had a paved airstrip.

Once again Johnny remembered something his mother had
taught them: "If you are in a situation you don't say *if* I can do it,
but you say I *can* do it and I'll be given the strength from the Lord."

He figured out what the compass and the altimeter were and did
as the pilot had instructed him. When he saw Prince George, he
noticed a fire truck below, and it occurred to him that now he had
to figure out how to put the wheels down. He thought, *If I get this
plane down without the wheels going down, it is going to be belly-up
and it is all metal and the sparks on that cement are going to cause
the biggest bonfire in the history of Canada—1,700 gallons of volatile
aviation fuel.*

But then, just as quickly, he prayed, *Lord, will You help me find
the wheels to get this plane down?*

He began meticulously to go over the instrument panel rows

trying to find something that indicated wheels. Once again he prayed, *It's all Yours, Lord. I'm asking for them, not me.* He then reached out, and can't explain why, for the last instrument that he would ever have thought of as controlling the wheels. All of a sudden, with the flick of his wrist, he heard the great hydraulic system begin to work and the wheels go into position.

Then he thought, *If I get down, no,* when *I get this plane down I am going to be taxiing down this runway lickety-split. How do I stop it?*

So he prayed again, *Please, please, God. . . .*

Later, he told his mother, "Mother, I could feel the tears in my eyes because I thought perhaps death was at the end of the runway for all of us."

He couldn't find a braking instrument on the instrument panel, but as he leaned forward, searching, his feet touched some pedals. Mary explains: "He didn't even know there were pedals, called rudders, on an airplane. And it isn't the balls of your feet that you use, but just the tip end of your toes and that's where the brakes are. Jerkily, before the end of the runway by just inches, the plane came to a stop. Another answer to his prayers."

Mary's son brought his father's body back to the States alone. She held him in her arms and together they comforted each other. She was able to tell him, "Johnny, I am very proud of you. Your faith saw you through. You cared enough to do what had to be done. We are our brother's keeper and you cared about your father and those men so much, that you asked in faith, believing, and you received a miracle."

The story made the newspapers across America and Canada. Mary had just finished her term as national president for American Women in Radio and Television, and she had toured the world to start the Congress of Women in Radio and Television, so it was on UP and AP—all over the world. National magazines came to interview her son.

When it came time for the memorial service, Mary chose not to view her husband's body. "I said good-bye to him a few days ago," she explained to her mother, the children, and friends. "We sat on the lakeshore—it was a beautiful, moonlit night, and the children were asleep in their sleeping bags. That night he said to me, 'When we get home there are a few things I have thought of that I need to do. But for now there are three things I want to say to you. First of all, we will have a will made when we return. Second, I will involve you more in our business affairs. The third thing is that I wish I had told you more often how much I love you. Why do I hesitate to tell you and the children how much I love each of you?' And so we talked long into the night.

"And that day, when it came time to say good-bye to my husband and the children's father, I told them, 'I am going to remember him with a smile on his face. And his last words to me were, "I love you and I'll see you in a week." ' "

Mary helped her children through this time of great tragedy in their lives. She helped them to understand that Christians don't sorrow as those without hope (1 Thessalonians 4:13). She urged her children to grieve in private, that this was right, good and necessary for their inner healing. And she was able to assure them on the basis of God's Word that they would see their father again in heaven someday because he believed in Jesus as his Savior.

"At times the agony was almost more than I could bear and then I would remember that the Lord never gives us too heavy a burden, one we cannot carry if we believe in and trust Him."

Moving Forward on Her Knees

There are those who would find it difficult to explain how one can move forward on her knees; yet, that is just what Mary experienced. "I cannot tell you how many times I had to go to my knees and cry out, 'God, I cannot go on alone! How can I meet all the bills and give these children the education they need?' But in the next breath, I was able to say, 'I will go on, I know You are supporting me in everything I am doing.' "

She did the necessary, practical, at-hand things that had to be done. "I sold everything. We had an entirely different life-style."

Mary and her children hadn't been left destitute by any means, but she did have to scale down. Still, she was able to put her daughter, Diana, through Harvard Business School—she received her master's there with honors. And Johnny went through USC; Ken, one of her twins, went to Boise State University and then to Brooks Institute of Photography in Santa Barbara; and Don, the other twin, went to USC and majored in business.

"While I was often overwhelmed at the responsibility of being both a mother and a father to our children, I did not despair. I knew that God was watching out for us." Her world, it seemed, had collapsed, but Mary went out and did the same thing she'd done as a young girl of eleven—she found a job. This time it was to become national public relations director of volunteer activities with the American Bible Society. There were many times when she couldn't figure out how to make both ends meet on a missionary's salary, but she compensated by lecturing and instructing at media workshops in a number of California universities and elsewhere. There was no lack of opportunity for her to speak for business and professional women's clubs, for state and regional conferences of Baptist, Lutheran, and other denominations, as well as to secular and business communities in many places.

During the next five years she coordinated media activities for the American Bible Society; she was the creator-producer-commentator for a seminar entitled "A Day With the Bible" attended by thousands throughout the United States, and she supervised these three-hour seminars in major cities. She moderated a number of weekly television programs and coordinated California subjects for the CBS filming of "Lamp Unto My Feet."

The Lord Giveth, the Lord Taketh Away

Mary Dorr's husband died at age fifty-two. He had just passed two physical examinations a month before the massive coronary that claimed his life. He had been told he was in perfect health.

In 1972, three years after her husband died, Mary's twenty-year-old son, Denny, developed a very bad cough. For him to be sick was most unusual. He was a surfer and loved to be outdoors. Mary had a loveseat in her bedroom that made into a bed, and her son asked if he could spend the night sleeping there. "I am just so weary, Mother," he said.

Mary assured him that they'd get to the doctor in the morning. She tells what happened: "When I went to wake him up the next morning, I found him to be in what I described to the nurse over the phone as 'a deep sleep.' I remember saying, 'His eyes are half open.' "

The nurse told Mary, "That doesn't sound good, I'll send the Rescue Squad."

The paramedics arrived, examined the boy, and told Mary he was dead and had been for four to six hours. She kept saying, "It can't be. He's only twenty. It absolutely cannot be."

But it was true.

And then, three months later, Mary's mother, who had always lived with them, also died. "I think she died of a broken heart," Mary says quietly.

Mary and her children grieved. Once again death had invaded their lives, this time depriving them of the presence and joy of a much-loved son and brother, and now Mary's mother and the children's grandmother. Now Mary found herself recalling Bible verses memorized as a child. Passages from the New Testament swept across her mind, bringing comfort, providing hope and reminders that to be absent from the body is to be present with the Lord (2 Corinthians 5:8). Through her tears—and she doesn't deny that there were many of them—Mary was able to say, "The Lord giveth and the Lord taketh away, blessed be the name of the Lord."

"I have four children left, and one is in heaven. Yes, we grieve much when we lose our loved ones. But God doesn't make mistakes."

Life Goes On

Two years passed, with Mary keeping busy—working, traveling, encouraging her children as they pursued their educations—and growing in her faith. Then in 1974, Religion in Media offered her the opportunity to become their executive director.

The work was a challenge. Among other things, she was responsible for creating, writing, producing, and syndicating programs for the media to be aired on public service air time. These programs range from "Personal Dimensions" (KABC-TV) and "Speak Out" (KTTV), seen in the greater Los Angeles area and carried by cable elsewhere, to many of the devotionals that open and close CBS network stations.

In 1977, after attending a Hollywood party and having a discussion with a noted TV producer, she got the idea that RIM should host an awards banquet. Almost everyone knew about Hollywood's Oscars, the Emmys, and the Tonys, and Mary felt it was time that "Angels" be presented to television programs, movies, radio shows, the performers and stars, and to books and their authors, as well as record albums and their artists on the basis of excellence in production and high moral or religious content. The idea caught on. Entertainment celebrities participate in the awards program as presenters—such well-known individuals as Dale Evans and Roy Rogers, Rhonda Fleming, Pat Boone, George Beverely Shea, Steve Allen and Jayne Meadows, Mary C. Crowley, Dr. Pat Robertson, Ralph Edwards, Art Linkletter. Winners treasure the Angels— winning an Angel is symbolic of having contributed something valuable to society.

Remarriage for a Great Lady

When personal tragedy first struck Mary, she was still a young girl, sitting at the bedside of her dying father. She remembers him opening his eyes and coming out of a deep coma long enough to look at her and say, "I love you."

"He was gone," she softly says. "But in that beautiful moment of insight it was as if I, too, had walked into heaven with him for a couple of seconds. I realized then that I would never, ever, be alone. Christ would walk side by side with me."

Then, years later when tragedy struck again, Mary experienced the pain of parting with her beloved husband. A few years later, even while she was still making the adjustment to that loss, death snatched away her precious son, and then her mother. She knew loneliness—the aching longing of wanting to reach out for these loved ones.

So it was that in 1980, when Gordon Gordon, a prolific writer of suspense novels and a longtime friend, recently widowed, asked her to share her life with him, Mary was ready for remarriage. "I knew Gordon and his wife so well. The two of them collaborated on twenty novels and I interviewed them after each one was published. They saw me through the death of John, my son, and my mother. Their empathy and sympathy were so great, and I loved them both so very much."

Now Mary is part of the writing team of "the Gordons" and they collaborated on the novel *Race for the Golden Tide,* which Doubleday published in 1983. Gordon Gordon has a long and impressive career as writer, editor, roaming correspondent for the Hearst newspapers, and as a 20th Century-Fox publicist, as well as being an FBI agent assigned to counterespionage cases. He is an award-winning writer and a number of his books have been made into screenplays which critics have described as being suspense classics.

Life has a way of going on and, the Lord willing, Mary and Gordon will be collaborating on many future projects in the years ahead. The woman "born to talk" has used her voice and witness in place after place, speaking of the faithfulness of a God who loves us and will use us when we commit ourselves to Him. Her conquering spirit has left an indelible impression wherever she has gone and in whatever she says and does.

4

Macel Falwell

Private Person,
Dedicated Homemaker

". . . it's not important what people say or what happens to any of us, but it's how we react that's important. If you walk with God, He will defend your reputation."

Almost everyone has heard of Jerry Falwell and the Moral Majority, but who knows his wife and her effect on him and their family? What is it like to live with the man who shakes political foundations and influences millions with his radio broadcasts, his television program, his print ministry, and *all* that he is involved in?

Macel (pronounced May sill) Falwell answers that question by relating a family incident: "When our daughter Jeannie was little, someone asked her what it was like to have a famous person as a father.

"She asked them, 'What do you mean? My dad isn't famous.'

"They responded, 'Yes, he is. He's an important man.'

"Jeannie looked them in the eye and came back with, 'Oh, he's not *that* important. Why, we have a boy in our class and his dad owns McDonald's. He's much more important.'

"That's a true story and it's just as true today as it was then. Jerry's never changed. He hasn't gotten bigheaded or become impressed with his own importance."

The Woman Behind the Man

As I chatted with Macel and her husband in their home in Lynchburg, Virginia, I got the feeling that what she was saying was true. The atmosphere in their home was one of relaxed informality; they weren't out to make an impression. The Falwells are just people —*real* people.

Jerry Falwell did mention that interviews are infrequent; they are something his wife does not usually appreciate. The press has done stories on the Falwell family three times during their marriage, but Macel does not seek this kind of thing because she feels it could be more exploitative than helpful.

Getting Macel to talk about herself wasn't easy. She admits she's a private person. Even her friends don't know a lot about her; they say she's a mystery.

"I enjoy the long hours I am alone, and when I am with a lot of people for several days, I have just got to have time to myself. During the day, I have the time while the children are in school and Jerry is gone. I don't travel with Jerry very much and it's by choice. Jerry calls home often when he is away, and I can just pick up a phone if I have a problem and reach him anywhere."

She found it difficult to understand why she should be selected as a "Living Cameo."

Unravelling the Mystery That Is Macel

What is obvious is that Macel Falwell is a homebody and she thoroughly enjoys their graceful Virginia home.

"The house is more than one hundred forty years old. We had a lot of work to do on it, but I enjoyed doing it so much." That was obvious; it reflected her good taste, beginning with the large front entry with its beautiful open stairway leading to the second floor.

She drew my attention upward to the ceiling molding. "In Virginia a hundred years ago, they would put a border around the parlor of whatever they raised on the farm. This was a wheat farm so that is a plaster border of wheat."

We moved on into the dining room with its adjoining sitting room. "When our family gets together at Thanksgiving and Christ-

mas, we have fourteen people. This little sitting room takes the
overflow. On a sunny day it's just gorgeous in here. There is a view
of the Peaks of Otter and the Blue Ridge Parkway. The sun sets right
between those trees. My daughter and I both love to paint—she's
better at it than I—and when we first moved here I would frequently
interrupt her studies and run get her to come in here and see the
sun setting. It is so beautiful."

Macel's appreciation for beauty also extends to music. "I like
music and I can spend hours playing the piano when no one is home.
My daughter and I love to play duets together.

"We lived close to a neighborhood church when I was a child, and
I would sneak in when the janitors were cleaning and go to the piano
and start playing, or I would go to the community center because
we didn't have a piano at the time. I would learn songs on my own.
I remember our first piano, one of those old-fashioned uprights. I was
twelve years old and started taking lessons then. I took lessons for
six years. I am still our Thomas Road Church pianist. I remember
the first time I played for a trio. It was hilarious, but I kept trying."

I had the feeling that Macel has always had that stick-to-itiveness,
in some respects that it has been a spirited pertinacity even though
everything about her might suggest otherwise. It would help to
explain why she takes all that has happened to her husband in recent
years so in stride.

Keeper of the Home

"Your home today," I observed, "it's large. I assume you have
household help."

"I do all my own housework. Some time ago one of our sons told
us about a girl who needed a job. I said, 'I don't need anybody.'
Finally, both he and Jerry convinced me to let the girl help out. She
was with us about six months and her work was good, but I couldn't
adjust to having someone in the house all the time. I like keeping
house for my husband and children."

The Proverbs 31 woman was known, among other things, for her
domesticity: "She looketh well to the ways of her household, and
eateth not the bread of idleness" (v. 27). While it is not an especially

popular concept among feminists for women to be "housebound," Macel Falwell could care less about such views.

"I'm with my husband and Phyllis Schlafly and others who recognize the feminist movement for what it really is—it's antifamily. No one can convince me otherwise. I know that not all women involved in the feminist movement are radicals; a lot of them are just uninformed, others are lonely. Still others have husbands who show little understanding and appreciation and they may not be home much of the time. That would be hard and impose a burden on a woman.

"A woman should be respected and accorded dignity; I know women who don't get that kind of treatment. My heart goes out to them, but the feminist movement and the equal rights movement isn't where it's at; that's not what's going to solve their problems. Women need to know Jesus Christ as Lord and Savior and be under *His* Lordship. Their homes need a husband and father who knows Christ, too, and who will take godly leadership. I believe the Equal Rights Amendment strikes at the foundation of our entire social structure. Now I'm sounding like my husband," she laughed.

Give-and-Take at the Falwell House

It's not surprising that Macel Falwell echoes her husband's philosophy. After all, she's been married to him for more than twenty-five years. But does she agree with him all the time? She was surprised that I even asked. "Does *any* woman agree with her husband 100 percent of the time? There are times I'll say, 'Jerry, I think it's just a little too much of so and so, don't you think?' This has been especially true in more recent years as he's spoken out on politics and issues.

"But he'll reply, 'Really? No, Macel, I think it was okay.'

"But the next time that particular subject comes up I can tell he did listen to my suggestion."

This give-and-take in the Falwell marriage has been a bonding strength. I was beginning to better understand why someone had referred to her as "a strong and invisible woman."

"I think that describes me," she states. "One of my friends paid me a compliment that I treasure. She said, 'Macel, telling you something is like locking it in a bank vault.'

"But no one is an island. Some of these strengths I've absorbed from my parents and Jerry. I think my father and Jerry are the most honest men on earth. I've been blessed to be around these two men who love me and from whom I have learned so much."

Six Years to the Altar!

When Macel first met Jerry, however, she wasn't so sure he could teach her a great deal. "When Jerry first began showing an interest in me, my mother cautioned me about him. So he not only had to win me, he had to win her. It wasn't easy!"

Since Jerry had acquired the reputation in Lynchburg for being somewhat rowdy, it took a while for Macel's mother to understand that this was just a part of his fun-loving nature. "When she finally did, she accepted him and loved him. Some of his pranks as a young man are quite legendary around here—like the time he drove a motorcycle through the boy's dorm while he was attending college—and his antics continue to this day. With Jerry, now it's a way to break fatigue; he uses his wonderful sense of humor to help himself and others unwind. He says most people take themselves too seriously."

She remembers the first time she laid eyes on Jerry Falwell. "I was church pianist at the Park Avenue Baptist Church and I remember the night he walked down the aisle and turned his life over to the Lord. Up until that time, I hadn't met him. He was tall and slim, sort of cocky looking. I noticed him after that—he always seemed to know who he was and where he was going. I guess you'd say he had a lot of self-assurance. He was in his second year at Lynchburg College, but after coming to the Lord, he lost interest in his engineering courses and, before long, he headed for Baptist Bible College in Springfield, Missouri, and a different kind of training. During Jerry's remaining years of college, he came home often and we dated. I broke an engagement to another young man. Jerry and I were engaged four years before we were married, having gone together two years prior to that. The Thomas Road Baptist Church was

started during that time. On April 12, 1958, two years after it began,
I married its pastor!"

Looking, Reaching, Struggling, Testing, and Growing

They say that the difference between mediocrity and greatness is
vision. Jerry Falwell, with his wife standing staunchly behind him,
was a visionary. Jerry's drive, determination, and dedication founded
the independent Thomas Road Baptist Church with thirty-five charter members in 1956 in an old bottling company building. Today in
the central Virginia city of Lynchburg an equivalent of 25 percent
of the population holds membership in the church Falwell still
pastors. In these years of leadership he has directed the growth of
an international television and radio ministry, a multifaceted Christian educational facility, and a worldwide missionary effort.

"It's a really large network now, with a staff that enlarges as the
needs emerge," Macel explains. She points to the newest endeavors—the Moral Majority and their new *Fundamentalist Journal*
magazine.

But neither Macel nor Jerry has ever forgotten the meager begin-
nings of the church. "We all pitched in and scrubbed away the soft
drink stains left by the Donald Duck bottling company plant, our
feet stuck to the floor," she laughs as she reminisces.

If you were to drive up to the Thomas Road Baptist Church on
a typical Wednesday night for prayer meeting, you would see an
average of four thousand adults streaming into the building, not to
count the more than four thousand college-age young people, high
school kids, and children going to services for their own age groups.

"We have five services on Sunday and Jerry preaches at three of
them, but moderates them all. And I am still the church pianist.
This is the way it's been since we were first married; the only
difference now is that it's all so much bigger."

The ministry has its own jet, so on Sunday mornings you will just
about always see Jerry Falwell in the pulpit, and Macel relates that
nine times out of ten he's there on Sunday nights, and at least eight
times out of ten on Wednesday nights.

Has the ministry ever interfered with their marriage? "Never!"

she emphatically states. "We both see to that. We take a month-long vacation in the summer, and we manage to get away for skiing in the winter.

"While I am the pastor's wife, the people know me well and understand that I don't like to talk in public and I don't like to be a public person, so to speak, and since I sort of grew up in the church, I'm accepted this way. They know if I'm asked to do something and I feel it will interfere with something involving the children, that I will have to say no. We have worked at seeing to it that we are not absentee parents."

Growth of the Falwell ministries has been fast, but according to Macel, "It's seemed gradual and hasn't really overwhelmed me because Jerry hasn't changed through all of it. He keeps the pressure off us as a family."

How does he do that? His wife credits it to the time he spends in prayer and Bible study. "He has developed the ability to privately give his burdens to the Lord and to walk away. This just makes common sense to my husband and, of course, we both know it is scriptural. So I think I've learned how to do this, too, and that's one of the reasons I value my time alone so much. I need it. I read, study, and pray and this enables me to be the wife and mother that is required for our household."

Handling the Anti-Christian Bias of the Media

How does she handle the media's criticism of her husband? What is it like to be the wife of a man who has been the subject of such distortion of the truth as was seen, for instance, in the 1980 elections when the media compared Jerry Falwell to Adolf Hitler and Iran's Ayatollah Khomeini?

"I don't pay attention to their cutting remarks. Jerry's political involvement is restricted to the moral and social issues—abortion, pornography, prayer in schools, homosexuality, freedom, the liberty to speak, to preach, and to freely assemble. These are the basic moral issues confronting our country. I have come to understand that he has to speak out on these things; that he would not be true to his calling if he did not. I'm so proud of him," she adds softly.

"Jerry has explained to me that when you look at history you see that this nation has more than two hundred years of history where ministers of the Gospel have had to stand up and speak the truth. Jerry says if more Bible-believing ministers don't speak out, they will have to stand guilty before God one day."

Macel is an avid reader and makes it a point to walk through the Falwell offices from time to time to look at the media clippings that concern the ministry and her husband. There are about three thousand clippings a week from across the nation. She still finds that mind-boggling! The more significant clippings that, in the opinion of the staff, should be specifically brought to her attention, are sent to the Falwell home.

"I just pray that intelligent, thinking people will realize that not all you read is true," she says with feeling. "People who want to believe the bad things will, of course, but our friends and those who know the ministry, and those who understand the tactics of the adversary, aren't going to believe everything they read or hear.

"Jerry says that if we will just live for God and walk His way through knowledge, through the real facts and the truth, the just will be delivered. Christians don't have to spend their time and their lives fearful of what people are going to say about them. You don't have to defend your reputation. If you walk with God, He will defend your reputation. The man who walks with God is indestructible."

Macel Falwell has absorbed the philosophy of her husband and his teachings. She speaks forthrightly, carefully articulating her feelings and the thoughts in her mind and heart. "In the final analysis, it's not important what people say or what happens to any of us, but it's how we react that's important. I've tried to teach this to our children too because I have seen them crushed by some of the things they've seen on the television news, or read in the magazines and papers."

She Majors in Mothering

The Falwells were married four years before their first child was born. Macel had gone to work at a bank after high school, and continued working right up until Jerry, Jr., was born. "Actually, I didn't want to quit. I enjoyed working. If I wanted to go back to work today Jerry would say to go right ahead although he believes mothers are needed in the home. But I have to be honest, I had never really liked children. I hadn't been around them very much and when I was home and company who had small children came to see us, I'd go off to my room and close the door because I didn't like to hear little kids fuss and cry. I probably had never even held a baby until I had my own!"

One of the things Macel and Jerry talked about before they got married was having children. "I really didn't want to marry a preacher," she confesses.

"I told Jerry why: So many of the pastors I'd known, and many I'd read or heard about, had lost their children along the way. The ministry had demanded so much of both parents that their children suffered."

Macel told Jerry, "I don't want that to happen. I never want to have a home like that. I want my children to have a real home."

She relates that Jerry assured her that after the Lord they would put each other's needs and the needs of their children next. "The children have always known this," she explains, "and consequently we don't feel like they've grown up resenting the ministry and the church."

Macel has a burden today to pass this knowledge on to pastors and their wives. She laments the high dropout rate among ministers' children, adding, "It doesn't need to happen."

I asked her to explain how they have achieved such family togetherness. I got some clues when I learned that daughter Jeannie has been taking piano lessons since age five and Jerry has never missed a recital. When Jerry, Jr., and Jonathan were active in sports he never missed a game.

Macel remembers that when Jonathan was just a little boy, the office somehow booked a meeting for Jerry on Jonathan's birthday (which is something they have agreed is not to happen). Jerry said to Jonathan, "Son, I'm sorry but I'm really in a bind. I've got this speaking engagement. I'll do one of two things—I can either give you the honorarium they offer me or I can stay home."

Macel says it didn't take her son long to make up his mind. "I'd rather have you, Dad."

She adds, "So Jerry sent a substitute and our son received the best gift a father can give to his son—himself."

Even though Macel wasn't particularly anxious to start having a family, once her first son was born, in her words, "I found out I was a mother at heart. I have enjoyed every stage of our three children's development. Jeannie was talking about some parents she'd overheard and they were saying they'd be so glad when school started in the fall, and she asked me if I'd ever said that.

"My husband overheard her and he answered by telling her that I'd rather be with our children than anyone else. I had never really thought about that, but I remember when the children were little and school would start after summer vacation that I'd sit at home the first day and just cry—I missed them so. I love being with my kids and we've always done so many fun things together."

Avoiding the Terrible Teen Problems

Nelson Keener, administrative assistant to Dr. Falwell, in speaking of the Falwells' relationship with their children, observed that he's never seen three teenagers as comfortable around their parents as the Falwell children. Macel took this as a real compliment. But that kind of a relationship doesn't just happen; it takes time and effort.

"I always made it a priority to set aside a special time for each child—it might be shopping, a fun outing, or just bedtime talking with each one. I always read to them and had private devotions with each child; now that they are older, they do this on their own. We still gather together as a family for Bible reading and prayers; these times are always relaxed and stimulating. Home is where the child first needs to hear about God; it's where the child needs to know he can always ask questions and expect to receive answers, he can be free to express himself, doubts and all. We've encouraged that.

"There's so much talk about teenagers and how horrible those years are. Parents say, 'If we can just get through those years.' I am so grateful that I can say I have enjoyed these years tremendously."

When the Falwells' firstborn became twelve, Macel took him aside and said, "Jerry, it won't be long before you become a teenager and there are a lot of problems you will confront, and I want you to know I understand. I have been there myself, and there were times I thought I would just die from situations that happened, times when I was so embarrassed, and times when I fell in and out of love, and I just thought it was going to be the end of the world. A lot of teenagers commit suicide even, they just can't handle the pressures. But I want you to know, son, that all these things pass. Six months later, maybe sometimes not even that long, you won't even remember what happened that made you feel so bad."

She has done that with each of her children. She remembers telling Jeannie, "I want you to know, Jeannie, you have somebody you can talk to. Don't keep whatever it is that bothers you all bottled up—the subject of sex, or whatever, anything you need to ask, just ask me."

Today, her youngest is well into his teenage years, and when she drops by his room she'll sometimes say, "Anything you want to talk over with me, Jonathan? Anything you need to ask?"

It's this kind of rapport and open communication with her children that Macel Falwell believes has helped them avoid the "terrible teen problems" so common to many families. "They always come to us after their dates, for instance, and just talk and tell us what they have done and where they have been. And our kids love to be home. They know they can bring their dates home."

She tells about the time she stopped by one of the children's rooms to ask if they had something they wanted to talk over or ask her, and this child said, "Yes, tell me, Mom, how do you kiss someone?"

Macel didn't laugh, but she admits she was surprised. So she described kissing as best she could. "Listen," she says, "I've explained everything to them. That's our job as parents. I've done the whole sex and babies routine, and I've talked about homosexuality and the problems with that in this country.

"We always monitor our activities and try to put our family first. Jerry and I listen to what our kids are saying. Something I treasure is this," and she pulled from her wallet a wrinkled piece of paper.

Before reading it she explained that she had been involved with the Virginia Federation of Women's Clubs and the General Federation of Women's Clubs. "It's in all fifty states and foreign countries. I started right after we were married. When Jonathan was six or seven I was quite involved. It was something Jerry wanted me to do. But one day I was home cleaning and I found this little note Jonathan had written to his cousin. I carry it with me as a reminder not to get too busy outside the home."

The little note that she shared with me read: "Kathy, I have to try to get Mom to quit her women's club. Look, you and me are going to do it tonight. P.S. I'll tell you how tonight. Your cousin, Jonathan."

Did she quit? "Yes," she says, "and that little note has always served as a reminder to me and helps me monitor my outside activities. I believe in community involvement, and I am involved in our Christian Academy. I also do quite a bit of counseling with women from the church who call me about problems with their children, or other matters. I am a pastor's wife, and I still visit with Jerry at hospitals and attend funerals. I feel a special need to stay involved with the older charter members." But she emphasizes that her family has always been her first priority.

There is one thing she has always done, however, that doesn't take her away from home. "Jerry and I spend as much time as we possibly can praying together about church needs and other things about which we are concerned. We do a lot of praying and reading together at night."

She always regretted that she didn't get to go to college. But in the fall of 1983, with two children in college and one a senior in high school, Macel took a leap into the dark. She enrolled as a freshman at Liberty Baptist College—taking a full load. Her family is thrilled. What will be her major? She isn't sure yet, but a new chapter has begun in Macel Falwell's life.

Melody Green

"Our God Is Sovereign ..."

"I don't have a full understanding myself, but I do know that I trust the Lord in all He chooses to do."

"Melody, tell Keith the plane just went down!"

Melody Green sat at her desk, the phone in her hands. Momentarily she was stunned. Keith had just left with eleven others for a quick sightseeing tour of the Last Days Ministries grounds and for an aerial view of Garden Valley and the other ministries located in the area.

Then she was on her feet, running, grabbing the car keys as she flew out the door. Keith was on that plane!

But as she ran to the car, off in the distance, above the tall row of trees at the end of the airstrip, she saw the cloud of smoke spiraling upward.

Later she was to learn that the plane exploded on impact. It had a full tank of gas and so it was an instantaneous thing. "There were only twenty seconds from takeoff to the time of the crash, so there wasn't time to do anything. There wasn't time for any of them to prepare, or to have gotten their lives right if that would have been necessary. I doubt that they knew they were going to crash until the last couple of seconds, and then they probably thought they'd walk out with a few scratches."

She talks about it with ease and a calmness that reflects her inner serenity. "I was in the office working on an article for our newsletter. We had some friends visiting us from Los Angeles. John and DeDe Smalley with their six children were on their way to Connecticut where they were planning to start a new church. They had never had a private airplane ride. It's so pretty around here that many times when people came through, Keith and our pilot would take them up and point out where the different ministries are located. It was supposed to be one of those short, ten-minute-or-so jaunts."

The plane was already full, so Melody, five weeks pregnant at the time, stayed behind with their year-old daughter Rebekah. Her foster daughter, eighteen-year-old Dawn, was across the road at their Intensive Christian Training School (ICT). But Bethany and Josiah, Keith and Melody's little son and daughter, were also on the plane.

"I got to the site as quickly as possible—it was straight off the runway, about a mile, but in an uncleared area of the woods and hard to get to. People started running to get there, having heard the explosion and having seen the fireball that shot into the air over one hundred fifty feet. But I was in the car and I wasn't the first one on the scene. It was of the Lord that I didn't get there while the plane was still burning. When I did get there all that was left was ashes. It took a few minutes to decide if it was really our plane, but I was sure, and then I had to tell everyone just who was in it. I came right back home and called Leonard and Martha Ravenhill."

Within a half-hour, others converged at the Green house—Tony Salerno from Agape Force, Leland Paris from Youth With a Mission, Jimmy and Carole Owens, and several others. "The house just filled up with people," Melody recalls.

Garden Valley, a small town in east Texas, near Lindale and Tyler, is the home of some of the country's most well-known Christian ministries including Dave Wilkerson's World Challenge, Youth With a Mission (YWAM), Dallas Holm and Praise Ministries, Leonard and Martha Ravenhill, The Second Chapter of Acts, and others including those mentioned in the previous paragraph. Now this community of Christian believers gathered together to share Melody's grief at this terrible blow.

Last Days Ministries was founded by Keith and Melody Green in 1977. It actually started out in their home in a Los Angeles suburb shortly after Keith and Melody came to the Lord.

Thirsty for the Truth

"We had been into Eastern mysticism, astrology, and different things, especially the metaphysical," Melody shares. "We were each looking for the truth in our own way before we met, but at the time I met Keith, he was looking into what he could find out about Jesus. We started searching together."

Keith Green was a musician and writing his own songs—he had been doing that since he was eight years old, and he had been performing them. "He was a child prodigy, his musical genius surfaced when he was very young," says Kathy.

God brought a little, old, Chinese man, Richard Gene Low, to Keith and Melody. He knew the Lord and through him they learned how to pray. "It was like we got hit by a ton of bricks when we started going to Bible studies every night at a place called The Vineyard. We were just so thirsty for the truth."

Keith's music changed when he came to the Lord, Melody relates. "There were songs about searching and then songs about finding. We have hundreds of his songs on work tapes that have never been recorded. Five albums had been recorded before he went to be with the Lord. A sixth album, *The Prodigal Son*, was released by Pretty Good Records in the summer of 1983, and at least one more is forthcoming in the future."[1]

After finding the Lord, Keith and Melody's lives changed totally. "We didn't add Christianity to our lives," she says, "Christianity *became* our way of life. The ministry started because we began to tell everybody about Jesus and began leading them to the Lord, and when they didn't have a place to go, we took them in. We ended up having a houseful in Woodland Hills in southern California. Actually, we finally ended up with seven houses full of people who had life-controlling problems with drugs, alcohol, and rebellion. It was a learning experience for all of us because we weren't that old in the Lord ourselves, and we needed to be rehabilitated too. I guess you could say the Holy Spirit was doing the rehabilitating. We didn't intend to start a ministry; it just happened by meeting a need."

As the people grew in the Lord, so did the scope of the ministry —and what began as a small house ministry developed into what is known today as Last Days Ministries. The Greens moved themselves and the ministry to Texas in 1979.

Melody Shares Her Feelings

"Keith and I were constantly amazed at the swiftness of the growth of Last Days Ministries. People who knew us in Los Angeles and who came to visit us here and who walked around were always in a state of shock—they knew it had to be the Lord because man couldn't have put all this together."

The "all this" she was referring to is almost five hundred acres of beautiful, gently rolling hill country in eastern Texas. There are large metal buildings housing printing presses, offices, and storage for the tens of thousands of tracts and pieces of literature rolling off the presses daily. There is a new cafeteria-worship center that seats eight hundred for concerts and lectures. There is the Intensive Christian Training School.

"We were acutely aware of the necessity for some sort of training school for those who wanted to serve Jesus full-time, and for those who want to come just to become better equipped to serve the Lord with all their hearts. We already had our hands full with what we were doing—especially Keith's concerts and our print ministry—but in January 1982 we began our first sessions at the ICT School, and they have continued and grown," she explains.

A major part of Last Days Ministries work is their album and cassette ministry. "Keith's message in music we know has had a powerful impact on people's lives—and continues to do so. His albums are available in bookstores, and we send them out directly from our warehouse, at whatever each person can afford. We have never wanted anyone to be excluded from receiving music ministry simply because of a lack of funds, and it has been a tremendous blessing to be able to minister to others in this way."

In addition, they have audio and video teaching tapes, representing men and women of God from different ministries worldwide which they share, making them available through the *Last Days Newsletter* and through Christian bookstores.

Keith Green died on July 28, 1982. When I talked with Melody in her Lindale, Texas, country home—a simple, rustic sort of place —in January 1983, she was amazingly open in sharing her feelings and thoughts.

"I don't know if it has hit me yet that I have lost my husband and two children. It is a gradual thing. I think when it is so sudden it is hard to believe it is real. I still sit here sometimes and think, I can't believe what has happened; or, it will hit me and I'll say, 'It is true,' but I haven't really grasped it. I think it will take a while.

"I guess the hardest thing is losing the children, because Keith and I talked a lot about what would happen if either one of us were to die because we were traveling so much. It was something we faced. But I was less prepared for the children to go."

In the early days following the crash, Melody did her best to cope, and about two weeks afterward, she went to Los Angeles to take part in a docking ceremony for the Youth With a Mission ship—the *Anastasis*—with which she and Keith had been involved. And she went to visit friends. "When I arrived everyone thought I needed some time to be alone and away from the demands of the ministry. They said I really had to have some time alone to grieve. I tried to spend time alone, but it was awful, so I have seen that busyness, at least for me, is good. I have enjoyed being busy with the ongoing ministry. I knew that God was still going to use this work He had entrusted to us, and I wanted to do what I could even while I was trying to adjust to the shock of not having Keith and the children around. I think the work has been the most healing thing of all. I am grateful. People lose family and loved ones every day, but when it hits *you* then it is different and the circumstances are unique, but you do finally realize that death is a natural thing that comes to everyone. I feel that I have been particularly blessed because the Lord has given me this work to do, an outlet, a ministry where I can be busy serving Jesus and find fulfillment.

"It was not an easy time, it's still not easy by any means, and without God graciously sustaining me, it would literally be impossible. The mother/wife part of me has been overwhelmed by my personal loss, but God in His infinite mercy brought me through it, and continues to do that, one day at a time."

To Sorrow Is Okay

Melody was not alone in her grief. There was Janet, the wife of pilot Don Burmeister, who, along with her two sons, Jon Karl and Erik, was also feeling the loss. And there were the families of the Smalleys in other parts of the country. In addition, Melody knew that hundreds of thousands of people around the world upon learning of the crash would feel, in her words, "deep grief in their hearts." And so she extended herself, reaching out to others through the newsletter published by Last Days Ministries. An excerpt from that said:

. . . I understand that you loved Keith with the true and lasting love that Jesus gives to those who worship Him. Jesus in Keith touched your life . . . and you will miss him. It does not show a lack of faith or spiritual strength to grieve for someone you love. The Bible doesn't tell us not to grieve—it simply tells us not to grieve as those who have *no hope* (1 Thessalonians 4:13). When Moses died, "The sons of Israel wept for 30 days, then the days of weeping and mourning for Moses came to an end" (Deuteronomy 34:8). My prayer for you is that Keith's death will in some way have a greater effect on you than his life—and that God will turn your sorrow into an abounding love for Jesus and an enormous burden for souls that will literally shake the foundations of darkness to their very core. I know that Keith would say, "Hey, *I'm* fine. Don't worry about me, just do something about those who are headed toward eternity without Jesus!"

I think it's important for me to say something about the circumstances surrounding the plane crash since I know many of you are finding it hard to understand. At this point I don't think I have a full understanding myself, but I do know that I trust the Lord in all He chooses to do. There is a lot of speculation about why the crash happened, and we may never really find out all the reasons for sure. But there is one thing I *am* sure of, and that is that God loved everyone on that plane much more than any of us did—and sometime between the time the plane got in trouble and the time of the crash, He was involved in making a big decision.

All of the adults on the airplane had a powerful and "right" relationship with the Lord—and even the youngest children loved Jesus in their own simple way. . . . They were all living witnesses of what it means to be a Christian, and they served Jesus with full and willing hearts. If Jesus says that not even a *sparrow* falls from the sky without the Father (Matthew 10:29), do you think He would let all of those precious saints perish without a glance? I really don't think so. We see things through our own earthly eyes, but God sees through the eyes of eternity—He sees through to the glory. Jesus tells us that life is like a vapor, but we don't really understand until death touches someone we love. God does not view death as we do. To those of us left behind there is a painful void —but to God, the death of His saints is a doorway to deeper and more intimate fellowship with the one He loves the very best. I'm sure Heaven rejoiced in welcoming these precious ones through her gates.[2]

Cruel Fate or a Sovereign God?

Like anyone else who has lost loved ones in a terrible and seemingly senseless tragedy, Melody had to deal with the basic question: Was this cruel fate or a sovereign God?

"When someone dies I think you do a kind of self-examination," she says. "*What if it had been me? Would I have been ready? Would God say to me, 'Well done, thou good and faithful servant,' or have I been wasting my time? Have I been living up to my full knowledge? Have I reached out to make a difference in the world?* It really makes you look at your own life and think, *If God called me like that, would I be ready to go?* They went into eternity as they were at that moment, with their lives as lived until that point in time.

"It hurts, it really hurts," she admitted, "and from our vantage point it seems so senseless, but we have to remember that our God is sovereign. We don't always understand His ways, but we must trust that His purposes are for the highest good."

The Lord gave Melody this verse from John 12:24 shortly after the crash: "Unless a grain of wheat falls to the ground and dies, it remains alone. But if it dies it bears much fruit."

She explains her reaction to that: "I am not a Bible scholar and I am not one of those people who are always getting words from the Lord or Scriptures to give to other people. But it was just all of a sudden that I thought of a grain of wheat. *Isn't there a Scripture about that, Lord?* I asked. *What does it say?* So when I looked it up I felt there was a message there and it gave me a small glimpse at one of the possible purposes of God for what had happened. I believe that the impact of Keith's death, and the deaths of the others, will bear much fruit in the multiplication of message and ministry to glorify the Lord and extend His holy kingdom here on earth."

A New and Powerful Message

Keith and Melody were, in her words, "so happy in the ministry God had given to us. But since Keith's death I have seen what he wrote and what he sang about now become relevant in a different way."

The vision Keith had for the ministry had begun to change, however, earlier in the summer of 1982 when Keith and Melody visited some overseas missionary bases. Keith himself had written that the Lord definitely had done something to his heart on that trip. Besides showing him how small his vision had been, Keith wrote that God began to give him a great burden to see the ranks of His army in the field swell.

Those words and the new and powerful message He gave to Keith Green were first published in their September/October 1982 newsletter which was already being prepared at the time of Keith's death. Melody explained that everyone at Last Days was extremely excited about the new vision, and they had joined together in making plans to bring that message coast to coast through Keith's concerts, during the remainder of 1982 and on into 1983.

"At the time of Keith's death, my immediate reaction was, *This is crazy, now what will happen to that powerful message? How can this further the mission's cause without Keith here to give that message?* That was a sad thing for me then, because I knew how badly Keith wanted to see everyone totally sold out to the Lord, or as he had put it in a recent concert, 'bananas for Jesus!' "

Shortly after the crash, Melody was told of a video taken of Keith in June while he was delivering his new burden. "Oh, how we rejoiced that God was so good in leaving us this part of Keith's heart to share with others. So we have been able to take *that* to memorial concerts in cities all across the nation."

Even though she was pregnant, Melody made it a point to travel to over fifty of those concerts held in civic auditoriums, university auditoriums, symphony halls, theaters, arenas, and large community complexes. The crowds filled many of these places to overflowing.

Last Days Ministries works closely with a number of ministries with short-term and long-term mission opportunities for those who respond. The memorial concerts give a "missions invitation" and thousands are already involved as a direct result.

Melody explains that the Keith Green memorial concerts are meant to remind people what is on God's heart as He sees our lost world, not to memorialize Keith. Therefore, these other ministries are invited to participate and to have literature displays and tables so that, in response to the invitation at the close of the concert, individuals can find the right information they need to get going in the direction God leads them. Some of those ministries participating are Operation Mobilization, Open Doors with Brother Andrew, Wycliffe Bible Translators, Calvary Commission, Youth With a Mission (YWAM), and Gospel for Asia.

At the San Jose, California, civic auditorium concert which I attended, the more than three thousand seats were filled to capacity, and it seemed that almost three-fourths of the audience rose to their feet in response to the call to rededicate their lives and to indicate a willingness to serve where the Lord would have them go. The audience was comprised largely of young adults. It was my personal observation that "much fruit" would come just from this one part of the country. I have been told that this same sort of response has been forthcoming in city after city across the country.

Melody feels that God has been and is in control of all that has happened. "The Lord has shown us tremendous fruit already from their deaths—we have received thousands of letters from individuals showing a new commitment to the Lord. Some of these people have written, saying they just realized that if God could take Keith, He could take them at any time. It's made a difference in their response to the Lord. I guess it was because Keith and the others were all so young, but death is not reserved for the old. It's made all of us reflect on our own lives, making us wonder, *If that had been me in that plane, would I have been as well received in heaven?*"

Welcome, Rachel Hope!

"My days aren't without a lot of pain," Melody said quietly that day we met in her home. She was, at the time, very pregnant. My heart ached for her, knowing she would go through the birth experience without Keith to hold her hand and coach her along.

"But the Lord's grace *is* sufficient," she insisted. "I have known and *do* know that 'Peace that passeth understanding.' God is refining my life. This is a time of tremendous growth for me."

Three months after our visit, on March 22, 1983, at about 3:10 P.M., Rachel Hope was placed in Melody's waiting arms. "The Lord gave me a beautiful eight-pound baby girl, and I just love every ounce," Melody wrote in the *Last Days Newsletter*.

"God has given me a tremendous blessing with this precious gift of life. Please pray that He will continue to equip me with all that I need to lead Rachel and Rebekah through this earthly life and on to eternal life with Jesus."

It wasn't long before Melody and her infant daughter were on their way to more memorial concerts. "The Lord has placed this burden on my heart to encourage people to really do something with their lives for the Lord," she says.

"Also, to remind them that they *can* do something, that the anointing and the power that Keith had are available to everyone if they will give their hearts fully to Him. God is looking for people who will say, 'Okay, Lord, I'll do what You say, help me to do it.'

"I want to continue to encourage people to seek the Lord and not to be afraid to step out, to keep that tremendous vision. Keith was a man of vision—he saw great things and thought big. He wasn't afraid to step out, and even to make mistakes. He made a lot of them and we all do, but he wasn't afraid to reach for a big goal.

"If we will lay all of our personal goals at the foot of the cross, and ask Jesus what He wants us to do with our lives, then I know Keith's burden from the Lord will be borne in the hearts of many —and will be carried to the ends of the earth."

Epilogue: Many thousands of letters came to Last Days Ministries and to Melody's attention as the news of the fatal crash reached the world. There has been a consistent theme in all of them typified by letters such as this:

> I'm sure there are thousands of people that feel as I do —that I have lost a good friend and brother in the Lord. My first reaction was to feel the challenge to live my own life to the fullest and pour myself out for others as Keith did, for his sake, so that somehow his life would be proven worthwhile and his efforts would bear fruit in the world. But I soon realized that my commitment should not be to Keith's goals, but to Christ and living life for *His* sake. It was *Jesus* who touched me through Keith, who was simply willing to be used as an open vessel for God to pour His love out to others. And Jesus has not left us. (Signed: C.B.)

---

1. Keith's albums are to date: *For Him Who Has Ears to Hear* (1977), *No Compromise* (1978), *So You Wanna Go Back to Egypt* (1980), *Collection* (1981), *Songs for the Shepherd* (1982), and *The Prodigal Son* (1983).

Juanda Huggins
From Something Else to Something Good

"God can take the brokenness and strife, and make something beautiful, something good out of our lives. I know, I've been there."

Twice a month the street in front of the Charles Huggins' residence in Fort Worth, Texas, is lined with cars. Lovely women step out of them and make their way up the walkway to the house. Some come in pairs, others come in groups of four or five, and some of them come alone. Some are laughing and chatting; some are silent. As many as seventy women will walk through the front door—one group on Tuesday night, the other group on Thursday night of the same week. As they come into the elegant entrance hall, they are greeted warmly by their hostess, Juanda Huggins. There are hugs, kisses, handshakes. Juanda is as lavish with her personal love for each of these guests as she is with the use of her home for this monthly Bible study.

Off to the left of the front hall is the beautiful dining room, and the women make their way around the table, filling their plates, admiring the floral centerpiece, commenting about the marvelous array of food the caterer has provided, introducing themselves to the new faces, expressing their appreciation and pleasure at being a part of such a gathering. They spill over into almost every room of the spacious home, carefully balancing their plates as they settle into comfortable chairs or seat themselves on the floor. There is an air of expectancy, you are caught up in it and find yourself thinking how good it is to be there. Before long, you know why.

As everyone gathers in the living room, Juanda sits where she can see their faces. Throughout the evening, as she speaks, she studies their expressions. The Bible is spread open on her lap. She's already seen to it that they received a satisfying dinner, now she's going to give them something that will last forever.

Juanda's story is not too unlike many others that could be told— women across this country who have opened their homes and their hearts and, in obedience to the Lord, have been teaching women from the Bible. She says, "I always make sure the women who are invited know that I don't teach doctrine or denomination, but the Bible is taught." The city, the surroundings, and the hostess-teacher are different, but the motive is the same. This is Christian love in action.

What Do You Do With a Nothing?

Juanda tells of shopping and bumping into one of the women who regularly comes to the Bible study. This woman had been telling her friend about Juanda and the monthly gathering. When she met Juanda, she turned to her friend and said, "Oh, LaVon, this is the lady I was telling you about whose lovely home we go to and have this buffet, and then she teaches us the Bible."

LaVon looked at Juanda and said, "Oh, Billie has been telling me how wonderful it is. But Billie is a Catholic and, well, to tell the truth I am a nothing. What do you do with a nothing?"

Juanda responded, "We just love you," and handed her one of her cards with her name and phone number.

Later, LaVon phoned Juanda. "Juanda, I don't know whether this is going to be the answer to what's missing in my life or not, but there is a great void in my heart."

Juanda told her, "You come, LaVon, come, and God will meet your need."

LaVon was in that group the night I was there. "She's been coming regularly," Juanda relates, "and she's learning."

Beauty-Shop Evangelism

But how did it begin? "For some time I'd been going into a certain beauty shop weekly and one day, Pam, the girl who did my nails, said, 'Juanda, you are different. I know you have problems, too —everyone does—but I've never heard you complain about them. You come in with a smile on your face.'

"Little did she know how many times I struggled to smile, because I certainly did have problems too. Especially at that time. And what she didn't know was that I was so full of pride that I wouldn't talk about my problems."

That day the young woman poured out her heart to Juanda and then added, "I have prayed and prayed and nothing happens."

The Holy Spirit was nudging Juanda and she knew it. Still, she silently argued, *Oh, God, not here!* But the feeling was so persistent, Juanda could not ignore it.

"Pam," she ventured, "I know you love your husband and son, and I know you are sincere, but have you really accepted Jesus as your personal Savior?"

Pam looked into Juanda's hazel-green eyes, and softly said, "You know I haven't."

While Pam continued doing Juanda's nails, Juanda was able to give her the simple plan of salvation. Pam had a background of some religious instruction, but she had strayed. Now, in the most unlikely of places, she invited Jesus into her heart.

"There are so many Pams out there," Juanda says with deep emotion. "After that, I was able to tell her that when we are children of God then we can ask Him to help us with our problems, and we have the assurance that He hears and will answer our prayers. But until we know God as our personal Savior, He doesn't hear and answer (Romans 8:14–17, 26, 27).

"That made an impression on Pam. Two weeks later when I walked in the front door she hollered from the back of the shop, 'It works! It works! God has answered my prayers.' "

Women in the shop turned and looked in amazement; they also listened as Pam spilled out what God had done for her. It was an incredible scene, but that was the beginning of Juanda Huggins's monthly buffet and Bible study, for that day Pam asked Juanda, "Do you ever teach just women?" She already knew that Juanda taught a Sunday school class for couples.

A Problem Child in Every Family

Juanda says in her own candid way, "There's a problem child in every family, and I was God's problem child at that time." Juanda had been teaching for a long time and had just taken a sabbatical because of some health problems. She admits that the last thing in the world that she wanted to do was to have a group come to her home to study and to be taught. But that still, small inner voice couldn't be silenced and Pam was persistent.

"Juanda, if you will teach us, I'll do the inviting," Pam said the next week when Juanda came in for her appointment.

In her heart, Juanda heard the Lord whisper, *And* I'll *do the inviting also.*

The group began in 1980 with six girls. "I dare say *I* have not invited more than three people," Juanda says. Today the group numbers more than seventy, necessitating a split, so they come two nights. "I teach the same material at each,[1] but now we have two catered buffets brought in. It was too difficult to communicate on a one-to-one basis with that many crowded in the room. Now, once again, I can more easily look into their faces as I endeavor to teach them what I feel God wants them to hear from His Word," she explains.

"Something Beautiful, Something Good"

At the time the group began, Juanda one day found herself humming and then singing the words to the refrain,

> *Something beautiful, something good,*
> *All my confusion He understood,*
> *All I had to offer Him was brokenness and strife,*
> *But He made something beautiful out of my life.*[2]

She knew the Lord was whispering to her again, in the way that *she* has come to understand is one of *His* ways of speaking to her: *That is the chorus for your little group of girls.*

"I was truly awed," she adds, "because the girls from the beauty shop work daily to make women beautiful, so this was such a natural thing for them to relate to. I had asked the Lord to instruct me and to give me the format He wanted used. The little chorus caught on immediately, and I have never in my life seen such a change in a beauty shop!"

Now the group encompasses women from *all* walks of life, and Juanda has a growing ministry helping women who have been in the grips of alcoholism, or who are struggling with the problem of living with an alcoholic husband. In any meeting you will find women going through the trauma of marriages in trouble, divorce, or the heartache peculiar to mothers whose children are straying. She even has women out on bail on murder charges and income tax evasion.

There Was a Time. . . .

Juanda Huggins can relate to these women and the diversity of their problems and situations because she's been where many of them are. There was a time when she thought she'd never see her husband again. It was World War II and he was overseas, leaving her behind with their six-week-old son. It was to be two and a half years before they were reunited. Hard years. Lonely years. Years when lovely young girls suffered in silence, crying into their pillows in the loneliness of the night.

While Charles Huggins was gone, Juanda grew up. From an insecure sixteen-year-old when they married, she became an independent young woman, holding down a good job, earning and spending her own money. When Charlie came home, it was to a different Juanda. "He had gone through a very heartbreaking, cruel, tragic war—fighting ten major battles in the Pacific, one right after the other, losing an eye—and was discharged on physical disability. We were both different."

Juanda had grown up in the depression days. "We were so poor we were what the poor people call poor," she recalls.

She began working as a carhop in a drive-in restaurant when she was only twelve. But she was innovative. From the time she was just a little girl, she had visions of becoming someone great. And she fantasized. "I dreamed of being like Ginger Rogers and other film stars. About my only claim to fame is that I was a good roller-skater and the local theater was holding auditions for some child to appear with The Little Rascals. I didn't know you were supposed to have some talent, so I signed up and tap danced on roller skates and sang 'Jeepers Creepers' and won! So I was actually in one of their movies."

Now she was no longer a little cotton-top kid, she was a lovely young woman with a small son and her husband was a navy veteran and there was stress on their marriage. She remembers only too well the years of wondering where the next dollar was coming from.

When she was in her early twenties, she became pregnant again. "One of these days I'll own my own machine shop," Charlie tried reassuring her.

She was no longer working and Charlie was holding down two jobs —working nights as well as days. In those days, Charlie rode the bus to work. Finally they were able to buy their first car, then a television, and their first house. They struggled along, but Juanda enjoyed being a mother. "I mowed the lawn, and once a month we got to go out for a hamburger."

She has no trouble identifying with the women who come to the monthly Bible study at her house. Her own times of struggle are a thing of the past, but what she learned in those years explains a lot about who she is today.

Restlessness, Partying, and a Good Neighbor

"We began to get a little restless in our marriage, and we met the young couples who were moving in on the same street around us. Many of them were party-goers and drank socially. My mother was very wise and cautioned me about this, but I resented it."

A neighbor, Margaret White, recognized a need in Juanda and Charlie. While they took their children to a local church occasionally, they only did it because they felt it was the thing to do. Margaret asked Juanda, "How can you go to church on Sunday mornings after being at those parties on Saturday night?"

When a couple of door-to-door Bible salesmen came to Margaret's house while Juanda was there, she was impressed with Margaret's ability to quote Scriptures rapid-fire. Later, she shared with Margaret her anger concerning Charlie's mother. Once again, Margaret's knowledge of the Bible came through. "How can you say you love God and hate your mother-in-law?" She quoted Matthew 5, which says if we have something against someone we are to be reconciled and make it right with them.

God has His way of carving out His living Cameos and this sensitive young woman, under the hand of the Master Designer, was to feel that cutting. It was a needful process, for underneath that determined exterior was an exquisite Cameo waiting to emerge. Sometimes God uses the most unlikely situations and persons as His tools. Margaret White had gouged deeply into Juanda's conscience.

Juanda stormed home angrily, thinking, *I'll bet that's not even in the Bible!*

She hunted around and finally found a Bible. She was so ignorant of the Word of God that she didn't know where to find the Book of Matthew. When she looked up the reference, she read it and quickly slammed the Bible shut. "I think I hoped it would disappear. But every day for two weeks I read those verses. I became so under conviction."

Then Juanda began to pray, reaching out to God, pleading for His help. Finally she reached the point where she could say, "God, I will go to my mother-in-law if you will just release me from this oppression." She went to her mother-in-law three times, each time experiencing rejection. The third time the Lord let her know that it was enough. She had done what He asked. "I was then able to put those feelings away." Juanda began reading the Bible—she had an insatiable hunger for the Word. "I would cook dinner with a spatula in one hand and the Bible in the other. I was just that hungry for spiritual food."

Transformed by the Power of the Holy Spirit

Juanda and her neighbor began sharing the Bible together and Juanda began to grow spiritually as she nourished herself in the Word. She and Charlie with their children began attending Sunday school and church at Bethel Temple in Dallas and came under the teaching of Albert Ott. "He was one of the greatest men God ever let live and he had what I would call a weeping ministry. The day he preached on the benefits of Calvary my spirit just soared."

Charlie and Juanda's mother were in awe as they watched the transformation take place in Juanda. Later Charlie told her that when she went to his mother three times he knew that God was doing something great in her life, and he also said he knew that it would take God!

Juanda's cup was running over. Transformed by the power of the Holy Spirit, she became a new woman in Christ. At first Charlie didn't fully appreciate or understand the change, but he accompanied her and the children each Sunday. "Honey, there is something I don't understand," he said. "I don't have that bubbling joy you have and that is what I want."

All she could tell him was to go to the altar and seek God; and that's what Charles Huggins did on his twenty-sixth birthday. "He made a commitment," she reflects, adding, "and God honored Charlie's faith and he also entered into the joy of the Lord. After that, we dedicated our sons to the Lord, and we've honored the Word of God in our home ever since."

Honoring God in Their Business Too

Charlie was in a business partnership and doing very well. He and Wanda became staunch tithers and givers to the Lord's work, but Charlie's partner resented their newfound faith. One night Juanda had a dream that Charlie had walked away from this partnership, and it disturbed her.

Two weeks later, Charlie walked into their home in the middle of the day. When she asked him what he was doing home, he said, "You remember your dream? Well, it just came true."

But it proved to be one of the greatest blessings in their lives. For two weeks Charles Huggins did nothing but think, read the Bible, and pray, seeking God's direction. He started his own business, but there were some lessons to learn. It wasn't long until it became an obsession with Charles Huggins to make money. "Before long it didn't make any difference how much he worked, it just wasn't doing any good, and so before we went completely bankrupt my husband closed the business."

It didn't take the Hugginses long to realize that if they wanted God's blessing on their lives, He had to be *first in all*. When Charlie was offered another business partnership, he entered into it with a new fund of knowledge that has never failed him. "God has been very generous to us, and it has come in some almost unbelievable ways," the Hugginses state, very mindful that it is God who has blessed and prospered them.

Today you will find three large and enterprising businesses owned by Charles and Juanda along with many real estate holdings throughout the greater Fort Worth area. He is a much-respected business-man in the city and in the business world.

Parenting: Joys and Woes

During this time of finding their way in and out of the business world, their third child, a darling little girl whom they named Cindy, was born. She was to become the apple of her father's eye, and in time this would cause problems for Charles and Juanda.

Their children grew up, married, and began having children of their own. Their firstborn, Charles Doyle, became a successful busi-nessman on his own, and also participates in running his father's main business. He is an elder in the Presbyterian church, and works with young boys in soccer competition.

"My oldest son and I had good rapport, but our second son, Mike, was always a little more distant in talking to either me or his father. He kept things pretty much to himself," Juanda says, "and I ob-served a growing restlessness in him, even after he was married."

This was an agonizing time in her life. Her health was under siege, requiring hospitalization and specialized care. Her heart broke every time she looked at Mike who was in his early thirties, "but looked fifty."

She began to pray for him more earnestly. One day she asked God to show her what her son's problem was, and God revealed to her that it was alcohol.

What mother wants to label her son an alcoholic? Juanda Huggins didn't! But she went to her daughter-in-law and together they acknowledged that this was Mike's problem. "For so long I had wrongly assumed that alcoholics were only the down-and-outers and fellows on skid row. How wrong we can be in our thinking! God had to show me."

Juanda and Cricket, her daughter-in-law, set about to learn everything they could on the subject. They called Alcoholics Anonymous and Alanon; they read; they attended meetings at treatment centers. "We checked into everything. So it was that in May 1982 we were ready. God had prepared us."

Juanda was preparing refreshments for a group coming in after church that Sunday evening in May. Her eleven-year-old grandson was watching her. When the phone rang at 4:30 p.m., he answered it, and then looked very puzzled. "Grandma, it's some man mumbling," he related and hung up the phone.

In a few minutes it rang again and this time Juanda answered it. "It was my son Mike. He was crying and I knew something was wrong. He pleaded with me to come and get him. Through his weeping he managed to tell me where he was. Charlie and I dropped everything and went to him."

They brought him home. "He was dirty, and he smelled of alcohol, but I never loved him more than I did at that moment," she states. "It was such a deep love—like a divine love, I guess. I wanted to convey that to him; there was no rejection, no criticism, no whys —just love. I think he felt this from Charlie and me. He cried and cried. I think they were healing tears."

Juanda's beautiful dining room table was set with crystal and china. All was in readiness for the party they were going to host after church that night. When Charlie and Juanda brought their son in, he didn't notice the preparations. They helped him up the stairs and lovingly cleaned him up, attending to his needs. Then Juanda told him she knew where he could go for professional help. He pleaded with his parents to take him right then, which Charlie did.

"We watched our son go through detoxification," she explains, "and it was very hard. Mike's wife and children stood by him, and we all went to counseling together for six weeks. This is very necessary and important when you are working with and trying to help an alcoholic. We all now understand alcoholism—it is a sickness, a disease. I feel certain it comes from Satan, and that people are bound by this. But we are so proud of our son and his progress. He knows we all love him and will always stand by him."

Today Mike Huggins is a different person. He works with his father, running one of the companies. "I am so thankful," he humbly says. "God has been very good to all of us."

Dealing With Pride

At first when this happened with her son, Juanda was tempted to question, *God, what have I done wrong?* A natural reaction, she believes, when something occurs in a family situation that seems so out of kilter with the way you've raised your children.

Now she emphasizes that she has come to understand that these things can and do happen. "But our children are never out of God's reach," she calmly states. Sometimes the influence of our parenting is blocked by circumstances, or perhaps by rebellious rejection, but God's parenthood of His wayward children cannot be stopped.

Juanda and Charlie also experienced their share of woes with their daughter, Cindy, who had two unhappy marriages, both of which ended in divorce. She had two beautiful children from those marriages.

The problems with Cindy were ongoing for eight and a half years. Much of that time the Hugginses poured thousands of dollars in her direction, hoping to help her and their grandchildren. Cindy was manipulative, threatening at times to deprive them of seeing the children. The day came, however, when Juanda took a stand and confronted her daughter with the fact that she would no longer be a party to Cindy's life-style.

Cindy went to her father. "The enemy can come disguised," Juanda cautions, "looking like innocence personified." Charlie felt he had an obligation to provide for his daughter and her children, even though he knew this was against Juanda's wishes.

"I finally told Charlie that God would hold us accountable. He knew how I felt, yet he was helping her behind my back. When I learned the extent of Charlie's generosity, I became furious, packed my clothes, and left." She headed for their vacation home in Red River, New Mexico, where Charlie later joined her. "It was a very strained time," she admits.

While there, she began reading Catherine Marshall's book *Something More*. Catherine tells of going through a similar situation with her stepdaughter. Juanda had gotten to the point where she didn't even know how to pray. She needed emotional healing and she needed it desperately.

"I was sitting on the porch and had just finished reading about Catherine's experience. I was looking at the faraway mountains and Catherine's words kept coming back to me, 'I had to love them just as they were.'

"Catherine wrote that it was hard to do, because you don't like what they are doing. I knew what she was saying. But God began to talk to me. I said, 'God, I can't do that.' "

The Holy Spirit was at work, and Juanda sensed that God was saying to her, "Yes, you can. You don't have to love what your daughter is doing, but you can love *her.*"

Juanda returned to Fort Worth and to her daughter. "Cindy," she said, "I've placed you in the hands of the Living God. The Scripture says it is a fearful thing to fall into the hands of the Living God, but that's where I've placed you, and I refuse to take you out of His hands. God has given me a promise: you will come back to Him and to us. I love you with all my heart."

Did things immediately change? "There were seasons of bitterness and some railing, but I was able to pick up my life and go on," Juanda explains.

One day Cindy phoned her mother and asked to have lunch with her. With tears streaming down her face, Cindy related that she had awakened at three in the morning, contemplating suicide, but as she lay on her bed, thinking how she could take her life, the thought came to her, *If God promised Mother that He would keep His promise to her, then He wouldn't let me die.*

Today Cindy is happily remarried; she and her husband have established a Christian home. At the altar, Cindy turned and asked her mother, "Can you ever forgive me?"

"Of course the forgiveness was there long before she ever asked," Juanda confides.

The Holy Spirit at Work Today

Is it any wonder Juanda Huggins is able to reach out with a heart and arms of love to embrace those who are so broken, needing love and help?

"Charlie has always been so supportive," she says happily, adding, "He is strong and stable. I could not do what I am doing without him. He takes these women and their problems as seriously as I do. They are our spiritual children. The Bible says, 'Cast thy bread upon the waters . . .' (Ecclesiastes 11:1). You can't outgive God. This has been such a beautiful thing in ours lives."

The stories she relates would *fill* a book, showing how God can take the brokenness and strife; He *can* make something beautiful, something good out of our lives.

---

1. She began by teaching them from the book *Creative Counterpart* (Linda Dillow, Thomas Nelson Publishers, Nashville) and the Bible. She has gone on to instruct them from the Word and uses other Bible-based materials. It is expected that the group will expand to more than a hundred.

2. SOMETHING BEAUTIFUL © Copyright 1971 by William J. Gaither/ASCAP. All rights reserved. International Copyright Secured. Used by special permission of The Benson Company, Inc., Nashville.

Dee Jepsen

Bridging Gaps in a Torn Society

"Christian women need to come to grips with what it really means to be a credit to Christ."

"God has His people salted—the believers —all over Washington, and I see Him answering the prayers of many people across this nation and, in fact, all over the world, because as America goes, so goes the free world."

The words are spoken with deep conviction, carefully chosen. They are hope-filled words, born out of keen observation by a woman who is more than just a bystander surveying Capitol Hill. She has been actively involved in the political scene over the years. Dee Jepsen is a daily participant in what is taking place in Washington, working as she does with her husband, Senator Roger Jepsen (R-Iowa). For fourteen months—from September 1982 through October 1983—she was special assistant to the president for liaison with women's organizations and other groups. She resigned that post in September 1983 to help her husband run for reelection in a coming campaign.

That appointment from the president came in September 1982, following closely on the heels of the defeat of the Equal Rights Amendment (ERA) leaving "liberated" and more "traditional" women seemingly hopelessly divided. Dee is both a conservative and a committed Christian. But while she served in that capacity, she was committed to bridging gaps between these two women's groups —something she still endeavors to do since, at heart, Dee is a peacemaker.

"I believe my commitment to Christ affects my ability to communicate with others and helps give me a perspective on life and on people. The secret to working together is mutual respect, and today is a time in our country when we need healing, not more hostility. That is very, very important."

Old Values and New Issues

"I knew when I stepped into that appointment that it wouldn't be easy. I know it's old-fashioned, but I feel there is such a thing as sacrifice and commitment, and that I made a contribution."

She was called "open, honest, and helpful" by some women's groups, who, although differing with her on some topics, viewed her as credible. Still others referred to her as "a sham."

How did Dee respond? When members of the National Organization for Women (NOW), and the American Association of University Women, for instance, pointed to the fact that she hadn't come out of the women's movement and hadn't dealt with women's equity issues, what did Dee Jepsen say?

"Of course the criticism stung, but I expected it. There is always criticism any time you step out and do *anything*. You just have to be willing to take those risks.

"Members of NOW have a different philosophical and political agenda. So when you hear criticism from that source (and others like it), you must understand why.

"I had limited contact with the more liberal groups in the past, but I know their concerns are very real to them, whether I share their views or not. What I was and still am interested in is fairness and equality.

"Beyond secured rights, women need recognition. There *are* women hurting out there, and I hurt for them. I would not want to make light of the fact that there have been some inequities in our system that have hurt women. But, I would add, even with economic success and having all kinds of material goods and career opportunities, if your inner attitude is negative, it will have an adverse effect on you and everyone around you."

Needed: An Attitudinal Change

She believes that some leaders of women's groups and some of their followers are "filled with bitterness," and that some of them are not in touch with the vast majority of American women even though they claim to represent American women at large. That charge has been leveled especially at the more strident feminist groups. Some of them have "pushed too hard" and "built up hostility" among themselves and have tried to foster this in American women.

The same charge in some instances can also be leveled at Christian women, the groups they represent, and their constituency. Dee Jepsen is not unaware of the peculiar problems Christian women encounter in their relationships, which are then reflected in their attitudes.

"We are not given the authority to judge," she reflects, "but we are commanded to love. And we are commanded to love even our enemies, and we should conduct ourselves to be that kind of women. If we are not, it makes us very open to criticism. Christian women need to come to grips with what it really means to be a credit to Christ."

Dee points to women who are undertaking new roles in society, and their right to choose the direction they wish their lives to take, and states, "But I would hope that in so choosing, they would be careful that they don't diminish their womanhood. I overheard someone say that next to God, we owe the most to women, first for giving us life and second for making it worth living." That, to Dee Jepsen, is nothing to be ashamed of.

Dee is of the opinion that government is responsible for creating a legal climate where barriers are removed so women have the opportunity to make choices. "Government is responsible for policies which create stable economic conditions that permit women to make these choices. If they enter the job market, they should be treated fairly in hiring, promotion, and salary." She emphasizes that the bitterness that is sometimes seen in women's reactions is not an answer to anything; it only creates more problems.

"So what we need now is an attitude change in our society. Women and men need to realize how really important women are. We need to recognize that women contribute immeasurably both to the home and to the work force—to the whole of society. The overall fabric of our society is, I believe, largely what it is because of women. They shape and mold the lives of our very young, who will be the leaders of tomorrow. Women are primarily responsible for transmitting our culture and our values. Women are vital not only to our homes and in the work place, but to the overall fabric of communities across this country."

She regrets that women have been made to feel guilty, or feel they have to apologize for choosing to be career homemakers. She was, by choice, for over twenty years. "I was just as fulfilled then as I am now that I am working professionally in public life. There are many times, in fact, when I wish I could turn the clock back."

But there is another side to the coin—those who choose a career shouldn't be labeled selfish, something that the Christian church at times has done. "They have not been too supportive of the role of the career woman," has been Dee's observation.

Dee Jepsen urges that the church focus more on lifting up women, recognizing and encouraging them to develop their talents in the proper order in harmony with their families and the world around. "God has designated a special place for women; often our spiritual leaders do not give recognition to this. God sent His only Son into this world through a woman who raised Him and loved Him and who was dear to His heart. Women touched Jesus' ministry and were a part of it."

Dee points to the fact that women have gentle and sensitive hearts, that we are the life-bearers; that we have sensitivities that most men do not have in such abundance. "We need to be lifted up. The church can help do that and, in so doing, help to bring about an attitudinal change in this country. It's needed. We need to have the importance of our caring natures reaffirmed by our husbands, our families, and society. We, as women, need also to reaffirm each

other." As Dee sees it, this would bring about tremendous healing
in our land.

Heightening Awareness of Our Worth as Women

Instead of creating a climate whereby women with one point of
view and women with another point of view drift into two emotionally charged camps, glaring at each other, hostile and bitter, Dee
Jepsen is working to help women value themselves and one another
with proper feelings of self-esteem and mutual respect.

"The bottom line is this—knowing who we really are. I believe
that comes from knowing that we are children of a creative God. He
is *the* basis for our identity. To me, that's terribly important.

"We aren't created equal in talents or abilities or appearance, but
we are created with an equal spiritual worth, and that's where we
need to look for our identity. If we seek our identity as a partner in
a corporation, it doesn't have any more identity than an identity as
John's wife or Mary's mother. That's not enough. The corporation
could fold tomorrow; John could die and leave you a widow tomorrow. Our children go away to school, get married, pursue careers of
their own, then where are we?

"By putting more emphasis and focus upon contributions that
women have made and are making in society, and how important
we are, we can help to bring about some of the changes that are
necessary. Women are the glue that holds everything together."

She points to women who have helped shape the thinking of
others and who have provided leadership. "We could go through our
history books for examples. And I wonder how many people realize
that Nell Reagan, the president's mother, was a devout Christian
who loved the Lord. The values she passed on to him are values he
is now espousing in public policy for our country. She contributed
far more to this nation than many women, myself included, who are
in the public eye today.

"You see that painting of Mother Teresa?" Dee pointed to a wall
of her office. "As an example of women I admire, I have to point
to her. I was privileged to sit at the head table with her at a luncheon

on Capitol Hill. I knew her by reputation to be a very humble woman. I looked at this tiny old lady. Her gnarled feet were shod in old sandals, and the gray sweater she wore had seen better days, but this humble mite of a woman came into that room and some of the strongest leaders of this country rose to their feet with tears in their eyes. Their respect for what she stood for was evident.

"It really struck me that this little old woman who loves God, and who loves all God's children wherever she finds them—and sometimes she finds them in the gutter—doesn't own a thing. She's never pushed for anything—no favors, no government hand-outs—all she does is love and give and serve. And God has honored that selflessness."

Dee emphasizes that the Bible tells us that God will use the simple to confound the wise. "Mother Teresa is a beautiful example of Christlikeness nationally and internationally acclaimed. But what's she done? All she's done is give of herself. That's enough. And isn't that what Jesus Himself did?"

A Veteran on the Political Scene

Moving into the pressure of politics was actually nothing new for Dee, wife of Senator Roger Jepsen, who was first elected to the senate in 1978. Prior to that, while living in Davenport, Iowa, her husband was elected to a succession of public offices which included being Iowa state senator and the Iowa lieutenant governor.

As the wife of a politician it would have been good politics for her to be involved in some worthwhile causes; but if that were her only motivation, it would have been out of step with Dee's commitment to be and do all that she could for the Lord.

She was involved in a group working to release Christians imprisoned in the Soviet Union; and she is presently on the advisory board of a group ministering to inner-city needs (called STEP—Strategies to Elevate People). For many years she served as a volunteer in her husband's senate office, serving as an assistant to him. And she has served on the president's task force on Private Sector Initiatives, encouraging volunteerism. And there have been other efforts through the years. Of particular interest has been her involvement with the weekly Senate Wives' Bible Study, a group she helped to organize in 1979.

"Things always move fast in Washington. It's like trying to get on a moving train while carrying a heavy suitcase in each hand, but the train never stops, and you are always on the run, trying to catch up," she explains.

Working to Integrate Tried and True Values

Where does Dee Jepsen stand on such issues as abortion or homosexuality, which is a major focus, for instance, of such groups as NOW who crusade for "rights for lesbians"?

Dee views homosexuality as "an aberration and a sin, a moral choice (like) being a thief and stealing." She stands on biblical ground. "According to their own literature, one of NOW's major legislative goals is securing legalization of lesbian rights, among other things the rights of prostitutes, too." NOW has about two hundred fifty thousand members which, if one is to be honest, you would have to acknowledge is *not* representative of the majority of American women.

If one were to believe everything the media says, you would have to conclude that the Christian alternative to the very liberal feminists—a view which Dee Jepsen reflects—is a minority view. Integrating tried and true values into the rapidly changing circumstances of our times and communicating those views and values to this culture is the challenge that confronts Dee Jepsen as she works in the Washington political arena.

She is a strong prolife advocate, but she does have this to say: "Women who are opposed to abortion (like myself) need to understand that there are many prochoice women who feel it's *their* duty to stand up for the right of a woman to control her own body. In this and other issues they have a right to disagree. *But so do we.*"

In addressing the abortion issue, she says, "I consider abortion to be the greatest moral imperative in America. It is my belief that the unborn child is truly a life, and we have no moral alternative but to protect life. Women should have the right to make a choice regarding their own bodies, but this cannot be allowed to threaten the health or life of another. This is the real issue—the sanctity and importance of human life."

She speaks of her concern over the "disposability" attitude that has seeped into our society—the idea that if life is not "convenient" or wanted by another, it is all right to snuff it out. "It is dangerous," she says, her voice betraying the emotion she feels. "I repeat, it is the greatest moral imperative we face.

"It is a fact, we cannot legislate morality, but *we must legislate morally,* that is, our country and our form of government are based on laws that stem from Judeo-Christian principles. It's a standard we have not always lived up to. However, it is a standard to measure our actions against. If we don't, there will be other 'standards,' that will amount to a belief in *no* moral absolutes."

When Dee was appointed to her position as liaison for women's groups, a reporter was dubious, saying Dee would probably allow her Christian values and beliefs to affect her work. As Dee looks back on her year as liaison with the Reagan administration, what does she think? "Well, I certainly hope I did let my Christian values affect my work, because if I did, then I walked in fairness. As a Christian, I see all people as being of equal worth and value, and I try to treat them with respect, even though I don't always agree with them. So I certainly do hope my Christian values and beliefs did and always will affect my work.

"Everyone is motivated out of their inner beliefs, and every piece of legislation that is passed is based upon some set of values, and people who claim that we should not legislate according to our value system are themselves showing *their* bias. They base their view upon the fact that we live in a pluralistic democracy. I would ask them to stop and think this through for just a moment."

Dee explains that a pluralistic democracy by mere definition implies conflict. "Whatever group wins elective office is going to have the power to promote policy that reflects their values and beliefs. This is part of our system. It is healthy. However, as Christians, we must make certain we work against ideas and policies—not people," Dee says, adding, "God gives us the grace to do that."

She emphasizes that as we become involved politically, we must remember we have a biblical mandate to be responsible citizens. "We must conduct ourselves in such a way that if we win victories, they are not hollow, that we have not discredited the Christ we profess allegiance to in the process. There will always be those who differ with us; I respect *their* right to have a different view, just as I would expect *they* would respect *my* right to my view. But it is very easy in our human nature to get all caught up, zealously, in a political cause and end up offending people and be a disgrace to the Lord."

Dee's Spiritual Turning Point

She is resolute in her beliefs, but also very sensitive to the needs of others who may hold to a differing value system. How did she attain this? "In 1970, when my husband was lieutenant governor, he got swept up in all the activities in the flurry of public life, and I could see his interests, which had been centered on the family, being centered elsewhere, and that scared me to death. He was gone a lot—traveling and working—and at that time I felt such a need and, I am sure, a loneliness, and the Lord brought circumstances together that really touched my life in such a way that I totally committed my life to Him. I knelt by my bed one evening, when Roger was out doing something I'm sure he thought was very important, and said, 'God, I need something and I need You. I will give You everything I have, body, soul, and spirit.' That was the turning point for me.

"I had always believed in God and even though I had a tiny bit of faith, God still seemed far away. God totally turned me around, and He has used the things that I feared and disliked the most to bring my husband and me closer together and to bless our lives."

Dee's family speak of her act of faith as a life-changing experience that showed in her relationships to everyone, and in her attitude and outlook on life.

The Right Woman for the Job

No stranger to difficult tasks, Dee Jepsen is more qualified for her present position than most of her opponents may realize. A *Washington Post* staff reporter, in looking at Dee's life, observed that while she doesn't have the customary law degree held by many women on the move in Washington, she does have something very significant to offer—her self-respect and the way she practices certain basic principles of living.

How did Dee acquire that? Her son, Craig, recalls the time when she told him, as a child, that the word *can't* was *not* in her vocabulary. He remembers how together they relandscaped the yard, "From leveling the ground to installing a patio and planting new shrubbery.

"I have a college degree and Mom hasn't, but she's got it so much over me. She knows what's important. She raised a family and instilled in them a sense of right and wrong that we can now pass on to our kids."

Dee Jepsen really believes the values she espouses. For example, daughter Debbie speaks of her mother teaching them the golden rule. "She always said people couldn't fight kindness, that it would freak them out."

"I got married young," Dee says softly. "That was a big mistake because four years later I was divorced and raising a baby daughter. I was born on a farm in Iowa. Mother died when I was thirteen, and I had to help take responsibility for raising my younger brother. I think I tried escaping by getting married.

"After the divorce, I held down two or three jobs at a time. It was a matter of survival. At one point I worked as a waitress. One day, a man who sold insurance came into the restaurant, ordered a steak, and then sent it back. He's been sending his steaks back ever since!" she laughs. "Roger and I started dating not long after I met him."

Dee inherited a family upon her marriage to Roger Jepsen. "We've been married now more than twenty-five years. I raised his four children as my own, and he adopted my little girl, and then we had a son together. At one time five of them were all age six or under. But mothering them has been such a blessing. When they were teenagers, Roger was gone a lot and I had a dual role to fill."

Daughter Ann recalls that her mother was "strict and big on organization. We all had our assigned duties. But she loved us all and she was always there."

Craig describes her as being "strong-willed and determined." He tells how she kept him on the straight and narrow: "Spankings!"

At one time Dee was even part-owner of a small business which she later sold when she decided it required too much of her time. From that experience she learned that she had business and marketing skills.

"There are many seasons in life," she remarks, "and during those seasons, the fulfillment may come from different sources. A child who climbs up on your lap, entwines his arms around your neck, and says, 'I love you, Mom.' What could be more fulfilling? A husband who says, 'I don't know what I'd do without you,' that's fulfilling. I believe as a person looks back, some of the best moments will be those that came as a result of good relationships with people— concern for them—and when you were able to give of yourself. What may fit a woman when she's in her twenties, may not fit when she's in her forties."

In that respect Dee Jepsen has lived out two different roles— single (divorced) mother and full-time homemaker caring for six children and a husband—and is presently into what might be described as her third season, as a career woman, active in politics.

Walking into Dee Jepsen's office was a surprise. It wasn't the typical executive's office; rather, it looked like something out of *Colonial Homes* magazine. It had a "sitting room" look with its patchwork pillows, tossed on the dark blue sofa. Bright shades of red in accent pieces throughout the room gave that homey feel. A patchwork quilt was folded on the back of the desk chair; there was even a braided accent rug on the floor. Many photos, autographed by the Reagans, Barbara Bush, Nancy Thurmond, Pat Boone, and others, graced the walls. Several of the paintings bore the signature Dee Jepsen (she is an *excellent* painter).

One painting in particular captured my attention—a young, old-fashioned-looking girl, walking up a winding path flanked by lush wildflowers of every hue. In some respects it reminded me of the girl who was once Dee Jepsen—lovely, idealistic, dreaming, and hopeful of the future as all young girls are apt to be. Did Dee skip through the Iowa fields, head thrown back, running into the wind, and dream dreams? Never in her wildest dreams could she have imagined herself sitting in an office in the White House complex.

What can be done by someone like you and me to help bridge gaps in a torn society? I asked that question of Dee.

Without a moment's hesitation she responded, *"Pray.* Pray for all of us who are involved in public life. When you are trying to live out your Christian faith on a very fast track you need lots of support. Pray that our judgment will be good and that our prioritization of items demanding our attention is right so we don't miss anything, and so we don't miss people in the midst of our hectic days.

"I am conscious of every letter that comes into our offices; I know there is life behind that letter—every one is important and it is hard to give enough recognition to each one."

Her days are filled with a variety of things and no two are alike. "If I did not have a deep, undergirding faith and belief that the Lord both precedes and follows us if we will commit ourselves to Him, it would be very difficult to face, not only my days here, but days on this earth.

"These are challenging times—crucial—and they can become scary, because we have come to a pivotal point, and the nature of man has not changed, but our weaponry and technology have changed, and we find ourselves in conflicts. . . . It would *really* be frightening if you didn't believe there was any power beyond yourself, or beyond mere man."

She refers to April 1980, when many hundreds of thousands of Christians came to Washington to pray and to seek God's forgiveness for the individual and corporate sins of this nation. "We participated in that. We all joined together, asking God's guidance for our nation, and for His blessing and guidance for our leaders. I believe that God has been answering those prayers; I sense that since then more believers here in Washington are stepping forward with a great conviction and boldness, and they are providing leadership to others who have been here but who have been more timid about voicing their beliefs.

"This is where our hope, not only for our country, but for the world, lies. The more you become aware of the problems in the world, the more you realize that it would be a very foolish man or woman who would say that man could get it together by himself. It is not possible. Now more than ever the world needs God; we need to tap into that spiritual source of power because that's where it's at. I know that God is in charge; He still sits on the throne."

8

Barbara Johnson
"In His Grip, Rejoicing"

"God makes gold out of our lives one way or another. . . . But while we are 'in the furnace,' it is important to understand we are there for a reason and that nothing comes into our lives but through God's filter. Whatever He sends, He gives grace enough for us to carry through."

Walking into Barbara Johnson's house is like walking into bright sunshine. The day might be dismal, gray, and cloudy, but once inside her "joy room," you are surrounded with brightness and movement.

"I like things that shine, move, chime, and make noises—stuff like that," she cheerfully explains with a wide sweep of her arms. "This is our 'joy room,' with all this cute stuff. Everything's been given to us. See this clown? Pull his nose and he laughs."

There are clowns of every description, size, and color to greet you, clowning around (pardon the pun) and adding their particular kind of brightness to that happy room.

"Someone sent this sign: WORK FOR THE LORD, THE PAY ISN'T MUCH, BUT THE RETIREMENT PLAN IS OUT OF THIS WORLD. We love it! Oh, see that butterfly and that fat mouse? Barney, our youngest son, made those."

My eyes were roaming fast trying to take it all in—the lighted, moving pictures, the train set, the white wicker rocker and settee with bright red cushions. There were stuffed animals, rag dolls, funny little toys, and catchy sayings and signs wherever I looked. On one door I saw a motto that read: LOVE SPOKEN HERE.

That's Barbara—not only does she have a room full of joy in her home, she also has one of the biggest, warmest hearts you'll ever find, and from it overflows a feeling of love, peace, and joy so radiant you are caught up in it. "The Lord has given such joy," she says, "it's impossible to contain it."

Where Does a Mother Go to Resign?

That joy was almost snuffed out many times. First she had to learn how to cope with the crippling of her husband, Bill. That was followed by the tragic death of her two sons. And then came possibly the heaviest blow of all, in the summer of 1975, when she discovered that son number three was into the homosexual life-style. Out of all that came a remarkable book, *Where Does a Mother Go to Resign?* [1] It recounts those experiences and how Barbara came up from out of despair and her feelings of being trapped, betrayed, and frightened. The discovery produced a host of feelings—guilt, anger, self-pity. "I felt ripped, wounded, and bleeding, with burning mental pain inside. It would, in fact, have been easier to lose my mind."

Waiting: In the Furnace for a Season

Barbara didn't lose her mind. She is a survivor. "God healed me so much of the pain of the problems, that today I can tell you I am thankful for what He has done."

Thankful? Yes, because Barbara chose to grow. Her life, as a result, has been a continuing growing process and a sharing of all she has learned and is learning. Through it all, she reflects that radiant joy.

Barbara and Bill Johnson have been through more than the average couple experience in a lifetime. "We've had four 'amputation situations' in our family—I am talking about emotional amputation. I know what it means to be an amputated parent, crushed and broken. There were times when Bill and I wanted to erase ourselves from the world, when we wished for the Rapture, or a bus to run over us. Wasn't there some simple way of disappearing—resigning from the world?"

Bill Johnson had been in an automobile accident in 1966, and Barbara was told he'd be a vegetable for life. He was severely brain-damaged. Actually, it was Barbara who came upon her husband lying in the middle of a winding mountain road. Bill had preceded Barbara and their two younger sons, Larry and Barney, to a Christian resort where they planned to supervise and chaperone a group of young people. It was a stormy night, and the road had been washed out in many places. Bill's car had flipped over on the treacherous road.

"But God remarkably healed him, and he is restored today and works as an engineer, doing beautifully, helping me with Spatula Ministry.[2] That was a very difficult time when my husband was so broken and shattered—physically and mentally. Out of all that, we learned that God delights in touching broken people and making them whole. God performed a miracle!"

At that painful time, Barbara came to understand that sometimes we have to live with mountains that seemingly will not move, but she discovered that we oftentimes do have greater reserves and resources than we thought possible. "God makes gold out of our lives one way or another—in the furnace of pain and suffering, or in some manner of waiting. But while we are 'in the furnace,' it is important to understand we are there for a reason and that nothing comes into our lives but through God's filter. Whatever He sends, He gives grace enough for us to carry through."

"Safe in the Arms of Jesus"

There was a time when Barbara couldn't have talked like that. She emphasizes that, *"it takes time."*

In 1968, Steve, the Johnsons' handsome eighteen-year-old son, joined the U.S. Marines. "The song, 'Safe in the Arms of Jesus,' was sung, and special prayers prayed for him in our church the Sunday before he left for Vietnam. In late July that year a black car with *U.S. Marines* on it pulled up to our house. I knew their message before I opened the door. Steve was 'safe in the arms of Jesus' now. No more suffering in the Vietnam heat, no more fear of capture, of torture. His turmoil and distress had ended. That same song was sung at his memorial service."

Barbara endured the pain of having to go to the mortuary and identify the remains of this precious son, who had lain in a muddy rice paddy for two days, and whose body was then en route home another ten days. "I experienced in that moment a pain and an isolation that was enough to last a lifetime," she reflects. "But our loss was heaven's gain."

Steve's tragic death marked the beginning of a ministry of sharing God's grace with other hurting parents, particularly those who were losing sons in Vietnam. "We had a quiet peace about Steve's passing that allowed us to share his faith. Vietnam was a long way off now, but we still read the list of names of the dead in the papers; now our purpose was to secure addresses of their families, to share Steve's memorial service, and the testimony of his life and death."

Five years later, in 1973, death was to stalk the Johnson home once again. "Our beautiful, twenty-three-year-old son, Tim, and a friend were killed by a drunk driver as they were returning from a summer of work in Alaska. Following that, in our confusion and anguish, we only gradually became aware that God had a plan to reach others with His love—people the boys couldn't have reached if they had lived."

This time, too, Barb had to go to the mortuary to identify the body (since the boys were killed out of the country). "As I stood in the mortuary, waiting to identify Tim's broken body, I was reliving an old, bad dream. This was the very same room, the same wallpaper, the same carpeting, the same everything—except here was another box with another boy in it. So unreal! How unbelievable that this could happen to us *twice*.

"I saw the shattered body and signed another paper. But God reminded me that this was not Tim. This was only his earthly shell. Tim was not there. And I began to see the glory in all this! It was as if I could look up and see Tim standing there, all bright and smiling at me, saying, 'Don't cry, Mother. I am here with Jesus. I am finally home! Don't feel bad.'

"We celebrated the boys' triumphant homegoing. We called it a 'Coronation Service.' I felt the grace of God wrapping around my heart. He was walking with us through this heavy, deep valley."

Barbara relates that the ripples made by Tim's death have spread far, touching many lives. "I still feel the ache of Tim's passing, and tears coming easily in spite of our rejoicing at his homegoing. But I'm so grateful that God allowed me to see that when Tim stepped through the doorway of death, he was just beginning to live. When that doorway opened, there was a shaft of brightness and warmth that drew many people into a closer relationship with God and an eternal friendship with Jesus Christ.

"So we had already crossed three big hurdles. Wouldn't you think that was enough? I thought the Lord was surely going to give us some clear sailing now. We had two sons left."

When *Gay* Became Something Other Than Happy

It was June 1975. Barbara and her family were anticipating a whirlwind weekend of Disneyland and Knott's Berry Farm fun with her sister and brother-in-law, who were flying into the Los Angeles airport en route home to Minnesota from a vacation in Hawaii. They were all to converge at the flagpole in Disneyland to enjoy the big Centennial Parade and all the ballyhoo that goes with the summer opening of the park. Barb had to meet her relatives at the airport at three o'clock that afternoon.

"That day, before driving to the airport, I had to run into our son Larry's room because someone had called about borrowing a book. Underneath this book was a stack of what I now know were homosexual magazines. At the time I didn't fully understand what they were—remember, this was when 'gay' still meant happy. I couldn't believe these magazines belonged to my son. He was a Christian boy, active in church and Bible study; in fact, he was preparing for Christian service. He was a model kid, no problems, and popular with girls. *These magazines couldn't possibly be his. He must be studying for something,* I thought."

But something had gone off in Barbara's mind, and she threw herself down on the bed and a terrible roaring sob burst from her. Fear, shock, and disbelief shook her and she was terrified. Her reeling thoughts were interrupted by the realization that she had to get to the airport. She hurriedly scribbled a note to Larry, reminding him to meet them at the Disneyland flagpole: "Larry, I found the magazines and stuff. . . . I love you and God loves you, but this is so wrong. Can we just get through tonight and, after the relatives leave tomorrow, talk about it? . . ."

She felt as if she were traveling alone through a trackless wilderness, her mind on automatic pilot with a steady whirl of *homosexuality, homosexuality.* She found herself asking: *Do Christians struggle with this? How can a Christian be a homosexual? Is it mental illness? Sin? Demonic? Is it an emotional breakdown?*

When Barb walked through the Disneyland entrance that night with her relatives, she heard the song "When You Wish Upon a Star." Once again her mind took off on a crazy tangent. She wondered if being homosexual would matter. *Can they wish on stars, too? How many homosexuals have come through the Disneyland gates? Maybe half the world is homosexual and I don't know it. If my own son could be one and I didn't know it, who knows who else could be? Maybe Mickey Mouse and Donald Duck? Tinkerbell?"* Suddenly, realizing that normal thoughts were absent from her mind, she had to pray to God to help her bring her thoughts into captivity.

Larry met his family that night at the flagpole, and when he and Barbara were out of earshot from the others, she looked into his eyes, brimming with tears, isolation, and fear, and heard him say, "I am a homosexual—maybe a bisexual."

Frantically, she grabbed this much-loved son and reassured him, telling him that nothing mattered, that she had meant what she wrote in the note, she loved him and would help him get through whatever was hurting him.

Can't God and Mothers Fix Everything?

A natural optimist, even in those moments when confronted with the most shattering, emotion-packed, devastating blow of her life, Barbara's mind was trying to balance the scale. She was thinking: *After all, can't God and mothers fix everything? Broken toys, broken dishes.*

Then, in the next instant, she found herself asking, *But how do you put a Band-Aid on a broken heart? How long does a broken heart stay broken?* Then she realized, "But we were at Disneyland where 'dreams come true.' This was not a nightmare, I was awake and not dreaming." The flagpole at Disneyland became for a long time like a grave marker to her. "It was here where a part of me died, but there would be no funeral for me because my body was still moving around. It was my spirit, my inner being, that was buried there at the flagpole, in the Magic Kingdom."

Before the twenty-four-hour period was up, Barbara's husband and her sister and brother-in-law knew what it was that had caused Barbara to look and act so strange. The gay life-style and all the ramifications of this were completely foreign to them. No one knew what to say or what to do.

Stuff a Sock in Your Mouth

Barbara drove her relatives to the airport and returned home to face the situation with her son. She had determined that with God's help she would show him unconditional love. She stresses that this is so important. "You love your child, but you hate the sin. Concentrate on love," she urges, "and letting God's love come through. Parents go into a panic immediately. I tell them to stuff a sock in their mouths—don't say anything until you can be loving and forgiving. To keep that child from fleeing and panicking, keep quiet except to reassure them of God's ongoing love and yours. If parents would do that, it would lessen the possibility of homosexuals going out and getting into deeper problems, and even killing themselves. The suicide rate among homosexuals is so high."

The morning after her relatives had departed Barbara found herself on the busy Southern California Freeway searching for help. If there are 20 million homosexuals in the world, she reasoned that there ought to be some mother who could tell her she was going to make it through this. "Tell me, where *do* all the mothers go?" she asked.

This quest for help took her from place to place, seeking an organization or someone who had answers. She wrote letters to every evangelical person she knew—especially to theologians she felt could provide direction. Surely there was some place, some person or program that was helping parents like her and Bill. One reply said it was sin—she already knew that—another that it was a weakness, still someone else wrote that homosexuality was a disease.

"One letter said if I would send my kid's shorts to Texas to be prayed for, that this would heal him. Well, I didn't know where my *kid* was, let alone where his shorts were." By this time Larry had left home.

"I had this whole collection of letters and stuff, but nobody provided the help I so desperately needed." Depression settled in like a heavy, blanketing fog and for eleven months after her son disappeared the usually cheerful, optimistic Barbara stayed at home. She wrote "survival notes" to herself, keeping a diary of sorts where she poured out her anguish. This later became the basis for her best-selling book.

Mothers Don't Resign

"There is no way to resign from this . . ." she wrote. "I am going to survive. I cannot allow the sin of one child to disturb my entire family. I will find out what this is all about and how to understand it—how to understand myself. How can one word like *homosexual* send waves of pain and nausea over me? I have survived death, accidents, heartbreak—why is this so different?"

She found a counselor who provided a measure of help and understanding, and she now counsels people to carefully search out such help, but she will also tell you that not all counselors, especially non-Christian counselors, understand the homosexual problem. Her counselor didn't provide answers, but she had found someone to whom she could ventilate her feelings. She knew that God was still alive and working and that He hadn't forsaken her and Bill. She began to pray, asking God to give her back her sense of humor in order to help her get through all this without losing her sanity. Her counselor had assured her that the humor was still inside her, like a percolating joy that one day *would* surface again. That provided a measure of hope.

In quiet and helpful ways, son number four and husband Bill, became a support system for Barbara. And friends undergirded the family as well. So it was that out of all this the ministry of Spatula began. Recognizing the need for parents of homosexuals to be able to get together in order to see that they aren't alone in their struggle, Barbara began referring to the meetings as a sort of "drain the pain" thing. A local church provided facilities for monthly meetings.

Barbara speaks of Spatula Ministries as "working with and helping people out of a lot of garbage situations. People are so fractured and hurt, and God just gave me a real love for these people, and I don't get tired. I have energy and joy and these are the two things the Lord gave back to me and that I need the most."

She explains that the name came about because they are, in effect, helping to scrape parents off the ceiling, which is where they land when they discover they have a child who is into homosexuality. "But husbands and wives land there too, when they discover their mate is having a homosexual or a lesbian relationship. Specifically, we pull them off with a spatula of love."

Spatula makes tapes and literature available. "We try to provide many areas of help for them and, of course, they have my phone number."

An Extension of Herself

When Barbara's book was first published, she allowed her phone number to be included in the story, not realizing that the book, in its first few years of publication, would sell more than half a million copies. "So people from all over ring that number," she relates. "They are usually crying when they call," she adds.

Barb's mother was visiting her one day and said, "Honey, doesn't anyone ever call who wants to just *talk* to you, you know, ordinary talk?"

Barbara's answer is choice: "No, they are just calling the lady in the book. Who needs to talk to me? They just want that lady who is going to say, 'I have been through it, and I can help you.' "

How does Barbara cope with dealing with people who are where she has been? "God gave me a windshield-wiper mind. When a person leaves our home and our joy room, or I hang up the telephone after one of their distressing calls, I just say, 'Lord, take your special windshield wiper and just wipe it away so I can love them and pray for them, and I don't have to carry all the pain they are going through."

There Is No Microwave Maturity

This helps explain how she handles the hundreds of telephone calls—calls, for instance, from a woman married thirty-six years, who is confronted one day by her husband telling her that all these years he's had numerous homosexual relationships; or the woman who, between sobs, spills out the anguish caused by learning that a son who has trained to be a medical missionary is into the homosexual life-style. "There are so many hurting people out there, all wanting instant relief. But we know there is no microwave maturity, only a slow growth process."

So she listens. And she provides Dr. James Dobson's tapes, or material that has proven helpful to herself and others. "There comes a time, like Abraham of old experienced, when he was told to sacrifice Isaac, that he had to say, 'God said it and I must do it.' We, as parents, confronted with the homosexual problem, have to say, 'I don't understand it, God, and it doesn't make sense, and quite frankly, I can't figure all this out.'

"God doesn't mind when we open our hearts to Him in this way. There is universal pain that people are going through."

The Number One Word: *Love*

The first time parents or individuals come to Spatula meetings, Barb says, they don't even want to reveal their names. "They'd just as soon put *Snow White* on their name tag. They're not willing to talk until they see some of the others who are a little farther down the road, then you can hardly keep them quiet. They want to share all their pain and the isolation and aloneness they've experienced. They need prayer, counseling, and they need someone who is like a warm, comforting blanket to tell them that God will bring them through this. They need assurance that God has done it for others. And we tell them we are not going to let Satan take these kids and destroy them."

Asked what kind of results they have experienced, Barbara is quick to point out that they can get 100-percent results with parents. "They come in looking like they've been through the wringer, but after a few weeks they begin to smile and talk, to trust God, and find out they are off the ceiling.

"With those into homosexuality—and they do come, too—it's a process of time. I have seen God touch their lives and bring them into a full knowledge of the Lord Jesus, focusing their thoughts on Him. When they do that, the other desires pass away. But the number one word for all concerned is *love*, unconditional love."

The Garment of Praise

Barbara learned that if she would put on ". . . the garment of praise for the spirit of heaviness . . ." (Isaiah 61:3) she could come out a winner. "I tell this to people and that they may have to live with broken dreams and a broken heart, who knows how long, but God, in time, will mend them. Their big concern, however, is for their kids (or their mates if they are into homosexuality). I have to tell them that only God can touch the homosexual's heart. And it does no good to kick your kids out. The 'gay church' will pick them up or the gay groups, and you may lose them for good. Kids have to be motivated to get out of the homosexual life-style. The person has to be willing. Many kids aren't motivated—they are afraid of loneliness and rejection. Those who do get out don't want to talk about it. They want to go on with their lives, and they fear that if they tell others they won't be accepted."

Barbara emphasizes that she is not the Holy Spirit and can't tell parents what may or may not happen to that loved one who has a homosexual orientation. "I do try to instill hope that they, the parents, are going to make it. It is a living death until they grasp that. Oftentimes husbands and wives will stop communicating with each other. Many times the kid will lay a guilt trip on his parents, blaming them. Many marriages suffer right at the time when couples need each other the most."

She finds that mothers, in particular, carry a tremendous sense of guilt and often blame themselves for producing this in the child. There are a lot of misconceptions. She was helped by Romans 8:28

and points others to that verse. "This is not simplistic advice," she insists, "because the Word of God *is* quick and powerful. When you can fully grasp that God causes 'all things to work together for good,' then it becomes like a soft pillow for a tired heart."

She tells parents to grieve because this is healthy. "We don't grieve as those without hope. I am not so far out of my pain that I can't say, 'I know how you hurt. . . .' But I tell them they will pass through these waters, and God won't let them drown (Isaiah 43:2)."

Barbara Johnson urges parents to pray much. "Getting down on your knees is a way of getting back on your feet."

Restoration

Since 1975 when Barbara made the discovery that her son was into the homosexual life-style, there has been very little communication with him, although some meetings have taken place. "The healing has been a long time in coming," she says. But early in 1983 Barbara, her husband, and son flew together to Hawaii.

"We were finally able to talk about my book and what I've been doing to try and help parents. He admits that he doesn't know anybody who has changed and come out of homosexuality. But he now says he doesn't ever want to live with anybody again, to have a relationship, that it is too painful."

At her March 1983 Spatula meeting, Barbara received, in her words, "a real happy surprise. Larry came to our meeting bringing a huge bouquet of flowers for me. He brought two friends along, and the three of them shared during the meeting. Hearing Larry speak about the growth that has taken place in the past few years and the insights he has had which, in turn, can help others mend their relationships, really was encouraging to the parents at the meeting."

In her monthly newsletter, Barbara wrote:

> We want you to know that we are rejoicing because there has been a restoration in our relationship. The word 're-store' means to 'pop back in place' like a bone that needs to be set. And we have been "popped back in place."

Barbara signs her newsletters "In His Grip, Rejoicing." Dark eyes brimming with love, she says, "We are just a warm hand in a black pit sometimes, and there are so many pits it seems. But we do know we are never out of God's reach—He holds us in His grip."

It would be wonderful if this chapter could end with my telling you that Barbara's son is healed of his homosexual problem and that all of this is a thing of the past—but that's not the case. The journey has not ended.

"Our son's coming to the Spatula meeting brought hope to other parents—we all saw that anger and hardness had disappeared, and in its place we saw a gentle spirit and an outflow of love. And that's where we are at.

"We are all on the journey to wholeness—some farther down the road, some have stopped at resting places, some are on a detour— but none of us has arrived."

In the meantime, you can be sure that Barbara is in God's grip, rejoicing, and that her son is in the grip of love as well.

---

1. Barbara Johnson, *Where Does a Mother Go to Resign?* (Minneapolis: Bethany Fellowship Inc., 1979).

2. Bill and Barbara Johnson began Spatula Ministries as a lifeline to hurting parents and others suffering the unique pain of knowing someone they love is into the homosexual life-style. For a copy of Barbara's monthly newsletter, write: Spatula Ministries, Box 444, La Habra, CA 90631.

9

Beverly LaHaye
She Found the Missing Dimension

"This beautiful, quiet peace settled in my heart. . . . I had a new power within me to do the impossible for God."

Beverly and Tim LaHaye had just fallen asleep in their Moscow hotel room. They'd had a long day touring the city and had taken in the famed Moscow Circus in the evening. When they finally reached their hotel room, they were exhausted.

"All of a sudden, I heard a key in the door," Bev relates. "That's a sound that wakes you up instantly, and I grabbed my husband. The next thing we heard was the doorknob turning and the door began to creak open. We sat bolt upright in bed, clutching each other. The streetlights outside cast a dim light in the room, just enough to see the figure of a uniformed, woman KGB agent. She walked to the front of the bed. We both began talking as fast as we could, telling her to leave our room. She just stood there looking at the two of us, turned, walked away, put the key in the door and locked us in again."

They had arrived in Moscow a few days earlier, thinking they were coming in as tourists, unannounced and unknown. When they left Austria, they were warned not to be surprised if they were met by a KGB man posing as a minister in the Baptist church. After going through customs, they heard someone call out their name. When the man introduced himself they recognized that this was the name of the man their Austrian informant had told them to watch out for.

"He took us to our hotel and knew exactly where we would be staying. From that moment on, our time in Moscow was monitored." They spoke at the Baptist church through an interpreter. It was both a thrill and a heartache as they looked out over the more than two thousand people jammed together. They couldn't mingle with them; moreover, they didn't see one child or young person at that service. They sensed that the people wanted to reach out to them as much as they wanted to show their love.

On their last night in Moscow, they told the man who had been hurrying them around that week that they were going to pass up the activities he had planned for them. They managed to elude him and took off for the Moscow Circus on their own.

The next morning they eluded him again, arriving at the airport well in advance of their scheduled departure, and later, when they arrived in Vienna, they kissed the ground!

That trip, in the fall of 1975, which had the LaHayes traveling in forty-two countries for nine months, and which took them behind the Iron Curtain, helped Bev and Tim understand just how much freedom is to be valued. "When you travel in countries where true freedom doesn't exist, you begin to understand how much you have to be thankful for," she states. "We traveled in five communist countries and made a commitment to God not to take our freedoms for granted—the freedom to worship, the freedom to raise our families as we wish, the freedom to go to and fro without being checked, and so on.

"We came back with a burning concern for our country. We believe American Christian women can help turn this country around," she says with conviction. "Ephesians 5:16 tells us we are to make the most of our time, because the days are evil."

Out of that conviction, an organization came into being in 1979 as the brainchild of Beverly LaHaye. The organization's goal is to alert and inform concerned women about the forces that are working to break down the family. As national director of Concerned Women for America (CWA), she has been involved ever since in all fifty states, drawing women together in a unified effort to protect the rights of the family.

Today, Bev not only works through CWA, but she and her well-known husband, Dr. Tim LaHaye, conduct Family Life Seminars around the nation. They also cohost a weekly television program, "The LaHayes on Family Life." Bev has also authored and coauthored at least six books on such subjects as rearing children, sex in marriage, and the Holy Spirit's role in your life. Ironically, one of her most popular books is *The Spirit-Controlled Woman*, which has helped hundreds of thousands of readers gain a new perspective on how to let God guide their lives and build their self-esteem. The point is that Bev wrote that book from the personal experience of moving from low self-esteem and lack of the Spirit's control to where she is today. She came from a poor background and had a very bad self-image, and hid behind her husband for more than fifteen years.

Pastor's Wife in Pumpkintown

"I was born in Royal Oak, Michigan. My father died when I was not quite two, and my mother remarried when I was four. We lived in Michigan all my childhood days. Unknown to me, Tim's widowed mother and her three small children lived in nearby Detroit." But Tim and Beverly didn't meet until their college days, when Beverly introduced herself to the young, dark-haired fellow sitting next to her in the cafeteria.

"Tim says he had come to dinner with a decision to date two of the girls around the table, me first and the other girl second. He started dating me and never quite got around to the other girl."

Tim's personality intrigued Beverly and their dating became serious, even though he told her he was planning to be a minister. That wasn't on her agenda of what she envisioned her life to be—she wasn't eager to be a minister's wife. "I wanted to be a traveler," she confesses, "and I had visions of being cooped up in a small community and never leaving town. But love does things to you and, sure enough, after getting married, the first thing we did was accept a student pastorate. I looked at those lovely people—real earthy—and they were as sweet as they could be and would have done anything for us, but I thought, *Lord, is the Baptist Church of Pumpkintown, South Carolina, where I'm going to be the rest of my life?"*

Parenting and Pastoring

Pumpkintown was not where they were to stay. Linda, their firstborn, came during that time, and then, in the providence of God, they accepted a pastorate in Minnetonka, Minnesota. This suburb of Minneapolis was to be their home for the next six years. While Beverly was getting more adjusted to being a pastor's wife, she and Tim were also finding out what it was like to fulfill the role of parent. Two sons, Larry and Lee, were born while they ministered there.

In 1956 they accepted the challenge to move west where roots were to go down deep into the San Diego, California, soil and the Scott Memorial Baptist Church was to feel the impact of Tim's dynamic expository preaching. The church grew fast and Tim was instrumental in founding the San Diego Christian Unified School System and Christian Heritage College. Tim's emphasis on practical Christian living attracted people hungry for truth, and the church was forced to plunge into two building programs in four years and eventually to expand to three Sunday morning services. While they were there, Lori, their fourth and last child, was born.

Interestingly enough, while Tim LaHaye could minister to others about the practical side of Christian living, he had some trouble in his own home, as did his wife. By the time they were ten or twelve years into their marriage, they had become two strong-willed personalities of the opposite sex who lived in the same house, who shared the same children, and held the same basic spiritual views and values, but disagreed on almost everything else. "Our story at that point was similar to that of millions of other unhappy couples," Beverly relates. "Of course, we always kept up a good front and did the right things."

A New Power Within

Up to that point Bev had lived in her little turtle shell. Her comfort was that she could go into church, sit in the pew, and pull into that little shell. "I'd pull my neck in and hope that nobody would talk to me or ask me to do something. If someone would tap me on the shoulder and say, 'Beverly, would you speak at a women's luncheon?' I would stick my little neck out and come up with one of my many excuses. It was just a pitiful way to be a pastor's wife."

She did teach a Sunday school class of little children because she felt comfortable with them. So it was that she went to a conference at Forest Home, California, to learn how to be a better Sunday school teacher. "Little did I know I was going to learn how to be a better *person,* and in being a better person, I would be a better Sunday school teacher."

Dr. Henry Brandt, a widely known psychologist, author, and lecturer, was speaker. He spoke about the abundant Christian life, and being filled with the Holy Spirit, and how one could have victory over fears, doubts, worries, and anxieties. *My word,* she thought, *what is this man talking about?*

Beverly LaHaye recognized that in *her* Christian life she wasn't experiencing all that he was talking about. "I really felt it was all the fault of the church. *They* wanted me to speak. *They* wanted me to entertain. *They* wanted me to teach a woman's Bible study. It was all just too much. So I went to Dr. Brandt and asked him if I could share my problem with him, and he agreed."

She was sure he would pat her on the shoulder and say, "My dear young lady, you do have a trying church to work in, don't you?"

That, of course, isn't the way Dr. Henry Brandt does things. After two minutes of Beverly's complaints, he interrupted and said, "Beverly, wait a minute. Do you want to know what your trouble *really* is?"

Still innocent and unsuspecting, Beverly replied, "Yes."

At that point, Dr. Brandt leveled with her, catching Beverly totally off guard. "My young lady, you are a selfish woman."

No one likes to be told they are selfish, and it was like a knife was stuck in her heart. But Dr. Brandt quickly went on to explain how he had come to that conclusion and he began to feed back her own words to Beverly. "When I heard them coming back, oh, it was as obvious as anything—I'd been telling him how everything would affect *me,* and nothing about what God could do with my life. I was, in effect, saying, 'What have I got to offer God that He could possibly use?' "

She also began to see that the fear that possessed her was not of God. "This was what I needed. 'For God hath not given us the spirit of fear; but of power, and of love, and of a sound mind' (2 Timothy 1:7). I needed that power, love, and sound mind to step forth in confidence and let God do whatever He chose to do with my life. It was such a revelation! Dr. Brandt helped me understand that this could happen through the filling of the Holy Spirit. I came to realize that I was wrong in not accepting myself as God had created me (Psalms 139:14); that I was a special creation from God's own hand! So I simply asked God to fill me with the Holy Spirit and to do a new work in me through this new power within."

No bells clanged and there was no outward sign or expression of change, but what was more significant, she knew in her heart that something had happened. "This beautiful, quiet peace settled in my heart and there was a new confidence that God was going to do something better with my life than I had been able to do. I had a new power within me to do the impossible for God. I found the missing dimension!"

From Bud to Bloom

Beverly's life was transformed. Her husband speaks of the transformation that began to unfold like this: "I have watched a beautiful rosebud, once confined by her own fears and anxieties, blossom out into a full-blown flower of poise, radiance, and Spirit-controlled confidence."

Bev can see now how she was limited because she hadn't let her life come under the transforming power of His Holy Spirit. "The Father will give the Holy Spirit to those who ask for this, and it is only through the help and control of the Holy Spirit that you can rid yourself of fear, worry, anxiety, anger—or whatever habit or emotion it is that is hindering you. I urge women to face these things in their lives, face them as sin. Romans 14:23 tells us that whatever is not of faith is sin. So we need to confess these things as sin and deal with them. 'If we confess our sins, he is faithful and just to forgive us our sins, and to cleanse us from all unrighteousness' (1 John 1:9). But don't be discouraged when you have confessed it and it comes back again—it is a habit. God understands that. Then ask for the filling of the Holy Spirit again."

So great was Beverly's concern about this subject, that in 1976 her first book, *The Spirit-Controlled Woman,* was published. It immediately rose to the top of the best-selling books list. Women around the world have been blessed because of Bev's dedicated writing efforts. In fact, the LaHayes' books are published in eighteen foreign languages.

"When I began to apply these powerful truths in my life, things began happening," she shares. "Today I tell women to ask themselves this question: If God hasn't given us a spirit of fear, who then gives it to you? When you do it that way it is kind of staggering because who wants to let Satan have that influence in her life?"

The Taming of Tim

When Bev was having an encounter with the Holy Spirit at that 1963 conference, so was her husband, Tim. There were areas in his life, he freely admits, that needed to be brought under the power and control of the Holy Spirit. Bev had phoned Tim and enthusiastically urged him to join her at Forest Home. Of course he didn't realize that Dr. Brandt had addressed Bev's problem already the first of the week. He arrived just in time to hear Dr. Brandt tell the story of *his* life. As Brandt spoke, Tim recognized that this angry, selfish hypocrite he was speaking about was none other than *himself!* He slipped out of the chapel and got alone with God. It was a life-changing experience for Tim, too, as the Holy Spirit filled him. "God changed our individual lives," she relates, "and our marriage, family, and ministry. Our joint bullheadedness and some of the individual quirks in our characters came under the control of the Holy Spirit and have been replaced by the love, joy, and peace that the Holy Spirit provides. Now my husband even calls me his dearest friend."

The Family Is Basic

Progress in the pastorate was even more pronounced as the Holy Spirit enriched and beautified the LaHayes' lives. Then in 1971, they responded to a specific call they sensed God was making upon their lives—the founding of Family Life Seminars. "Spirit-controlled family living is the only way to live," Bev says, "and we knew we had to share this with others" (2 Corinthians 1:4).

For the first several years Tim teamed up with Dr. Henry Brandt and Dr. Howard Hendricks in conducting Friday evening and all-day Saturday seminars in various cities. Then, when their children were all in college, Beverly was free to travel with him and to share in these seminars, including the world tour mentioned at the outset of this chapter. Their convictions deepened on that tour and are, in fact, firmer now than ever.

"We relate principles of the Spirit-controlled life for families, and this has been a great blessing and challenge to us. Tim and I had never been perfect parents, but we'd done the best with the knowledge we had, so we share that, all based on biblical perception. People seem to like it; they empathize." In these seminars, Tim and Bev don't pose as experts, but simply as parents who have been over the hard road of experience.

"If we could go back and do anything differently in raising our children, the thing Tim and I would do is teach our children to memorize greater portions of the Word of God. 'Thy word have I hid in mine heart, that I might not sin against thee' (Psalms 119:11). What a protection this affords from the world. We teach this in our seminars. I cannot emphasize enough the importance of providing that biblical foundation in the home.

"In 1975–76, the year of our sabbatical, when we traveled in communist countries, I was appalled to find out how few people had a Bible. If they could have memorized some of the Bible when they had one, it would be so good for them now. American parents need to be hiding the Word of God in their children's hearts, and in their own hearts for that matter. We don't know what tomorrow is going to hold."

Beverly LaHaye is very concerned about the women of America

and their important role as wives and homemakers. "My word to young mothers (young couples) is not to be restless in raising your children—this is your priority at this time in your life. After your children are raised, God will place you at another level in your own development. Be the best mother you can possibly be to those children while you have them at home. Society doesn't help us, and if we, as parents, are going to listen to what the media and the world is saying, then you begin to question and become dissatisfied. Soon you are thinking, *I have no individuality. I'm* just *a homemaker—a mother of runny-nosed little children, and I change diapers and pick up after my kids all day.* But you fail to look down the road to realize the full effect of your mothering on these children who will grow up to be adults. Oh, how important that mothers seek first of all to please the Lord."

The Secret of a Happy Marriage

Is there some secret Beverly has learned that can help to insure a happy marriage?

"Yes, it is to have a servant's heart. But this is on both sides. If either is obsessed with a selfish attitude, generally it is not going to be a happy marriage. Resentment sets in, and bitterness. A servant's attitude in marriage is best accomplished by learning to walk in the Spirit. In other words, there must be that day-to-day commitment to Jesus Christ; it is basic. Couples who come to us for counseling are not walking together in the Spirit."

She spoke earnestly of the need for couples to communicate with each other. "A lot of people who don't communicate are, to some extent, cowards. You see, they don't want to face reality and talk things out. It's easier (they think) to retreat into stony silence."

Tim and Beverly point out that they are actually dissimilar in personality—she is a morning person, Tim is a night person. She loves classical music, but it is a distortion to him. Football is his passion. She has learned to like it.

"When we got married, Tim was a football fanatic, and I couldn't handle it. When dating, he took me to football games and to symphonies. After we were married he asked me to go to a football game and I said I would rather not. Now I am a football fanatic, but I have to admit Tim still isn't too high on classical music. But we appreciate each other's differences now; the differences should be a complement rather than a wedge."

Another key to a happy marriage, as underscored by the LaHayes, has to do with honesty. "In order for couples to grow, we urge honesty. We do caution, however, that if the honesty is going to be hurtful, evaluate it carefully, it may not be necessary. Some honesty that hurts is good, but be very sensitive to your partner's ability to receive what it is you are saying. Tim has helped me most by building me up, helping me to gain the confidence that I can do what I need to do. It is so important that we be supportive of each other as couples. Tim is my strongest admirer and supporter; that's as it should be between couples. He enjoys my successes; I enjoy his, too.

"We believe that selfishness is at the root of all marital problems. I cannot emphasize enough that when you disobey the Scriptures you are going to have chaos in your life. The Bible has a lot to say on how we are to treat our husbands and how they are to treat us."

Now the World Is Their Parish

As Tim and Bev shared their discoveries of what it takes to have a happy marriage, the work became so demanding that there was soon an inevitable conflict between his pastoral duties and getting out to do the seminars. In 1981, Tim decided his pastorate at Scott Memorial Baptist Church in San Diego should end and that he should go full-time into the Family Life Seminar ministry. On New Year's Day, while driving to Los Angeles, Tim turned to his wife and said, "Honey, I would like to share something with you that has been on my heart. I think God is leading me to resign the church. What would you think about that?"

He expected her to object and to become very emotional about it, but God had quietly been preparing Beverly for this moment for one year, although she had remained silent about it. "It's about time," she responded. When he asked her why she hadn't shared it with him, she was able to tell him she didn't want to influence his decision. It had to be between him and the Lord. "He worked it out in his heart and did resign that month," she relates. They had been at the San Diego church twenty-five years.

In addition to their seminars, the LaHayes devote much time to their "LaHayes on Family Life" weekly television program. This is an outreach that now, in a sense, makes the world their parish.

And, of course, there is her ever-widening outreach through Concerned Women for America. Is CWA achieving its stated goals? The facts speak for themselves. "Our goal has always been to have half a million women in the next few years in America joining together in what has already been referred to as a giant, unified network to speak out on those things that are affecting us as families. We are very close to that goal, and the numbers are changing daily in all fifty states where prayer chapters have been organized. The national office sends out monthly prayer alerts so that these women have prayer *and* action together on a local as well as a national level. And these prayer chapters can be alerted at a moment's notice so that at any given time a great mass of women can be praying on any given issue or concern. We believe that when Christian women are praying in masses about the same specific prayer requests God hears and answers those prayers. That is biblical. We base it on 2 Chronicles 7:14. 'If my people, which are called by my name, shall humble themselves, and pray, and seek my face, and turn from their wicked ways; then will I hear from heaven, and will forgive their sin, and will heal their land.' "

Feminists of America state that they are speaking for the women of our country. How does Beverly LaHaye feel about that?

"It isn't true," she emphatically states. "They represent just a small group who have been very vocal and who have captured the attention of the media. But they are *not* speaking for all the women of America. So someone had to stand up and speak out for Christian women. Christian women have not had a front or a voice to let their desires and their convictions be heard. Our Christian beliefs are under attack; we don't have to sit back and let this happen. We cannot and we must not."

Concerned Women for America and their national director believe the hope for America, along with working to get proper legislation and the right men and women in office, and to keep informed on issues, is the prayers of God's people. "That's why we are working so hard to launch fifty thousand prayer chapters at the local level," Bev explains. "Our motto is 'Protecting the rights of the family.' God instituted the family; as women we must raise our voices to protect these rights. If women believe in the power of prayer, then we invite them to join us in this effort."[1]

A Servant for Christ

She wanted to be a traveler. Today she says, "My dreams have been fulfilled in ways I never expected. Our travel agent estimates that I probably travel close to two hundred thousand miles yearly. It goes back to that verse, 'Delight thyself also in the Lord; and he shall give thee the desires of thine heart' (Psalms 37:4). I look back now and realize that traveling for travel's sake isn't exciting. Now I travel with a purpose and I love it. By traveling to minister to people, I am getting the desire of my heart *and* the opportunity of ministering."

As she travels and as she ministers, Beverly has a message that has been increasing in its intensity the last several years. She speaks with great conviction, words that come from a heart overflowing with love and concern.

"Do not be swayed by the voices of the feminism movement. They say they speak for women everywhere, but they are not speaking for Christian women. I cannot emphasize this enough."

Beverly LaHaye, the child of low self-esteem who found a missing dimension that changed her life, believes that today's Christian woman is faced with tremendous challenges, opportunities, and responsibilities.

She says, "First of all, know what the Bible says, know why you believe what you do believe. You've got convictions; then find out why you have those convictions. Support them with Scripture. If they are God-instilled convictions, then can you remain passive and *not* do anything about them? And then, allow the Holy Spirit to work in your life. There is a missing dimension in the feminist movement; it is the Holy Spirit. I have found that missing dimension, and I know how this changed my life and what the Holy Spirit will do for others."

---

[1]. Write Beverly at this address: Concerned Women for America, P. O. Box 82957, San Diego, California 92138. An office has also been opened in Washington, D.C.

Cathy Meeks

"Suffering Is Not a Terminal Condition"

"I am thankful now that I have come to know that suffering is not a terminal condition."

It's a stimulating environment in which to work—the faculty of a well-known eastern college. Being the thinking woman she is, Cathy Meeks needs that kind of stimulation.

She went to Pepperdine College in Los Angeles, graduating with a B.A. in Speech Education. Then at Atlanta University in Atlanta, Georgia, she received her master's of Social Work. At the time of this writing she is working on a Ph.D. in psychology and African culture at Emory University in Atlanta.

This kind of preparation enabled Cathy Meeks to become a part of the faculty at Mercer University in Macon, Georgia, where she coordinates their Afro-American studies program. Cathy brings much to that position, not only because of her educational credentials, but also—and this may be more significant—because of the quality of her life and the varied experiences that have been hers.

But while it is stimulating work, it's not all glamour and excitement. "There are no shortcuts to wholeness. Now as I counsel individuals I have to tell them that; I can only share the insights I've been given. The one sustaining factor in my life or yours is that God *is.* That is a reality that provides hope.

"The point is that it is important *not* to take shortcuts on your journey to personhood," Cathy emphasizes. She stresses that trying to be spiritual instead of relating honestly to yourself and others will almost kill you. "There's nothing wrong with being spiritual; I believe in spirituality as a gift. But the gift needs to be cultivated; it can't be manufactured."

She points to Jesus, who was so very human. "He cried and was lonely. Sometimes I don't make it home from work before the tears start to fall quietly from my eyes."

She reflects back to her childhood, when she cried herself to sleep night after night. "But the tears didn't relieve the anguish in my soul. I am thankful now that I have come to know that suffering is not a terminal condition."

When she says that, you sense she knows a great deal about suffering. Cathy is now in her late thirties. What kind of suffering is she talking about?

Sharecropper's Daughter

"My family of six lived like sardines in a three-room house in Moro, Arkansas, a sleepy little town of 189 people. If you have not lived in poverty, then the plight of my family will be difficult for you to understand. But I do want to try to explain what it was like. At times the pain of being black and poor was more than my father could bear, and he would become very hostile toward us, the people closest to him. I suppose we were the only ones he dared show how he really felt about life. Because we were not able to understand his behavior, it caused all of us much anguish. My daddy was a sharecropper until his death in 1962. I've often wondered if he hadn't really died many years previously, when he lost hope for himself and us.

"Perhaps I should explain what sharecropping is so you can better understand why we were so poor. A sharecropper works for a white landowner and splits the profits with him, but because you have nothing when you begin, you must borrow for the year ahead. At years's end, you pay the landowner back from your profits, and then you have to borrow again to get through the next year. You are always in debt, it's as much a part of life as breathing."

Now, as she reflects on her daddy's behavior, Cathy can understand that he was afraid for himself and for his children. He wanted something better for them because he'd been hurt and disillusioned so many times. Cathy is of the opinion that sharecropping is merely a glorified version of slavery, a means of keeping people dependent and in bondage.

"The tiny house we lived in left much to be desired," she explains. "There were cracks in the floors and in the walls and the rats knew where they were. I will never forget the heartache I experienced after working so hard in the cotton fields, and being able to buy myself a bra and a slip. I put them in the bottom drawer of our old dresser. When I went to put them on, it was to make the horrifying discovery that the rats had chewed holes in both of them."

Cathy, her two sisters, and her brother slept in the same room and in the same bed. "I wished so many times for a room of my own. I will never take for granted my cozy, five-room apartment that I have today. Most of my family memories relate to hard times, and I learned a lot about fear—the fear of starvation, freezing to death, or being left without parents constantly haunted me even in the best of times."

She Still Seeks the Simple Life

Cathy, who came from the simplest of backgrounds, and whose life-style today could not possibly be considered extravagant by *any* means, now speaks about seeking ways whereby she can structure more simplicity into her life. "Trying to live a simple life is not easy. The way I live a balanced life is to keep my thoughts focused on the only One who can give any of us the proper perspective. It takes a lot of redirecting of the will and discipline."

To accomplish living a more simple life-style, one of the things Cathy did was to learn to sew and to shop for sales so that she could be creative in putting her wardrobe together. "I remember for a long time how much I wanted to be affluent. I suppose it's a dream all poverty-stricken families share. But one of the things I wanted was pretty clothes. What I finally learned was that I could be an attractive person without spending my entire paycheck on clothes. We women are daughters of a King, so as princesses we have no business looking tacky while representing our Father."

As a child, daydreaming became a way of life for her. While this is true for many children, and this is the way it has always been, Cathy suspects it's especially true for black children or, for that matter, white children born into poverty, because they own nothing but dreams.

Cathy daydreamed about a better day—a day when they would have decent clothes, more food, and a house that didn't leak or have rats. She dreamt about getting away and about her daddy changing. "These were my constant fantasies. But daydreams are like sunrises —sooner or later the brightness of reality makes you realize that your world is not the one you were dreaming about. I had no way of knowing how many years were to pass before those dreams would begin to come true. It's a good thing I didn't know. Escaping is not easy when you have nowhere to go."

How then did Cathy escape and how did she cope with her insecure and confusing world?

"Mostly through reading and listening to the radio. I would talk Daddy into buying a newspaper every now and then, and I'd read every inch of it. Hearing about the outside world on the radio gave me hope, and then I also listened faithfully to concerts from the Metropolitan Opera Company and the New York Philharmonic Orchestra. I could also lose myself in work and there was always plenty of it! Even when I was a child, my day would start about six-thirty in the morning and usually not end until nine-thirty at night. Another way I coped was to read our old, dusty, worn, and mite-filled Bible. And then we had an aunt who gave us some Bible storybooks.

"Early in the morning while the rest of my family still slept, I would get up and go sit on the splintery back steps, and think by myself while smelling the dew-dampened air and the honeysuckles. Somehow I felt comforted by the songs of the birds and the fact that the sun kept rising in the sky. It was there that I first began to hear the knocking on my heart's door from the One who would later enter as the lovely Guest."

The more she read and learned about Jesus, the more she talked to Him. She wondered and asked Him if He could do any miracles for her and her family. But there were many times when she wondered why the warmth of the beautiful morning sun couldn't warm her heart and make the world better. She soon learned that wondering didn't help.

"As I reflect on it now, I realize that from the earliest years of my life, God has been nudging me along, directing me. All of life is really a journey. It still remains to be seen where I am ultimately going, but I feel like the attitudes and feelings I have about my life in particular and the world in general were beginning to be shaped in me when I didn't even know what was going on."

A Mother's Influence

The desperate plight of the Meeks family didn't keep Cathy's mother from working to make her own dreams come true. Cathy speaks with pride of the fact that her mother was a part-time college student for eighteen years who finally graduated with a B.A. in education the same year Cathy finished high school. "She simply refused to believe that she couldn't make it. She would work in the fields and in the house, and make quilts and clothes, wash clothes, make soap, feed us, and meet our needs as best she could. Then she'd catch rides to night classes with my uncle or anyone else who was taking classes. To this day I marvel at her tenacity. I learned from her that hard work is okay; it doesn't hurt you and is even good for you. I also learned from her that education was really important. I learned all these things in a nonverbal way from both my parents.

"Even then, as a mere child, I understood that even when there seems to be no reason for breath to keep coming through your nostrils or for the sun to keep rising in the sky, life does go on."

When she was thirteen, Cathy was baptized. It seemed to her that this was a reasonable response to Jesus' love, and a little seed of faith was born. She attended a typical rural, southern black church, but she hated the noisy atmosphere and what seemed to be a performance at times by the pastor and other times by the people in the congregation who wailed and carried on in very emotional ways. "I understood even then somehow that the people needed a place to be somebody, and church provided that place. They didn't know it, but they already were somebody to God. He knew their names; He loved them. For my part, however, I found God to be more real when I sat on the back-door steps and just talked to Him."

From Faith to College Campus

She was fifteen when she went to live with an aunt in Junction City, Arkansas, so that she could go to high school. It was a turning point. She even had her own room! Six months after her first year of high school, Cathy's father died.

Following graduation from high school, Cathy journeyed to California to live with her half brother and attend a community college in Compton. Reflecting on those days, she states, "Only a God of mercy would be kind enough to reveal just one day at a time. How could we stand it if we had to see far into the future?"

Her first year of college was a nightmare. Not only was she unprepared academically, but she quickly learned that there was more to the world than their little Arkansas farm. The revelations were frightening. It took all the courage and ingenuity she could muster just to get around. One of the better things she did for herself was to enroll in a speech class so that, even while grappling with changes, she began speaking with the school forensic team on tours to such campuses as UCLA and Cal State Los Angeles.

Somehow, the determination to survive and make something of her life kept surfacing just enough to keep this young woman going. It was a doubt-filled journey. Her world had expanded so quickly and she wasn't prepared to handle it. Added to her burdens was the continual pressure of having to hold down one or two jobs at a time and pursuing her education in the evenings. It was tough plodding. When she finally made an appointment with a doctor to determine the cause of her exhaustion—physical and emotional—it was to learn that she had to undergo surgery to have a goiter removed.

She felt betrayed and bewildered, and wondered if Jesus had forgotten all about her. She didn't understand any of this, and she didn't have the money to pay for the hospitalization and surgery. She felt very much alone.

"The Lord seemed to be going to a lot of trouble to teach me that being a Christian didn't mean I would escape hardship. I did know He promised in His Word that, 'Lo, I will be with you always.' I decided I'd cling to that and give up at the same time. But the sustaining force in my life was a very special gift God had given to me, and I guess I've had it all my life. The gift is *tenacity*. As I explain it today, tenacity is 'the ability to hang on to the rope even when there is no knot at the end of it.' Because of His mercy and this blessing of tenacity, I was going to make it."

The Theology of "Giving Up"

The theology of giving up is seldom easy for us humans to understand. The idea of giving up scares us. Cathy was scared. "I guess God will do anything to help us realize there is no security except in Him."

About this time she also had to make a move and found an apartment closer to campus. "The apartment was farther from my work, but I wasn't looking for heaven on earth; I was just trying to survive."

She did recognize that in some unexplainable way her life was being moved closer to God; there was a deeper level of trust in her heart than she had ever experienced before. "No one had to teach me the theology of 'giving up,' or any theology for that matter."

The churches she'd attended hadn't taught her some of the things she needed to know that might have helped her in this particular juncture of her journey. "But the Lord was teaching me Himself, through circumstances and experiences. I did learn that He could only perfect His strength in me when I was willing to relinquish or 'give up' my weaknesses and problems. The scriptural principles behind all this came many years later."

Entering the hospital for surgery was one of the best things that could have happened to Cathy. Her surgeon turned out to be a brilliant black doctor with whom she had great rapport. When she awoke following the surgery, in her words, "I felt as if my life had been given back to me." Three months later she went to work for the surgeon.

What a blessing this turned out to be! Now she was making twice as much money as she'd made on any previous job. "God never took His eye or His hand off me. He kept on being faithful and opening doors for me when all the paths seemed to be blocked. Out of that, I learned that my little seed of faith was going to be nurtured by my gift of tenacity regardless of how many weeds of doubt surrounded it.

"Much of my life seems to have been characterized by a cycle of death and resurrection, this process of 'letting go.' I have concluded that the only way to live in peace is with open hands. Open hands, you see, can't hold on to anything. It is very clear to me that God doesn't intend for us to cling to anything or anyone but Him. I have struggled long with these truths; my struggle isn't finished because I'm still on this journey with Him."

Servanthood Becomes the Saints of God

Cathy's next step in the eventful journey of her life took her to Pepperdine College. Now she was faced with an additional personal responsibility—taking care of her emotionally unstable thirteen-year-old sister, Irene. Irene was not well and the Arkansas doctors could not diagnose her case. This sister was to spend half of the next two years in the hospital or at the doctor's office while in Cathy's care.

Now, in addition to the pressures of her job, the adjustment to a new school, and having her sister to care for—and always the burden of wondering where the next dollar was coming from—Cathy sensed that God was calling her to serve Him in a very special way. "Personal problems do not excuse us from being servants," she emphasizes. "This is another theological truth that I experienced long before I was able to articulate it."

There was tremendous racial tension on college campuses in the late sixties. As a black student, active as a leader, Cathy participated in many discussions and debates. When a young black teenager was tragically shot and killed on campus, Cathy, being the person that she is, became involved. The entire event molded her thinking to yet another degree.

She was not the type of person who becomes involved in a cause just for the cause's sake. She explains her reaction in this way: "I wondered what the Christian faith had to do with this whole struggle. What did *God* want of us? Our agenda as Christians must include more than militancy. This was not an easy issue to resolve."

What did Cathy do? "I prayed a lot during those days." And she responded by visiting the teenager's mother, a woman whom Cathy describes as "living in unending despair." Following that, she and other blacks on campus joined together to seek out some of the school administrators who were committed to truth.

"My outlook on social causes started to develop during those days, but my involvement could never be based on any humanistic myth about saving the world. Saving the world is God's job. My job is to go when He calls me and to do what He tells me to do. He called me in the sixties and I went in His name.

"During those days I came to realize that people are more important than institutions, that honesty and courage are more important than expediency, and that there is only room for one God in one's life. This stance during this campus tragedy greatly contributed to my 'new way of seeing,' and today I thank God for it."

As she thinks back to those days, Cathy asks a serious question and answers it in her own magnificent way. "It is extremely difficult to assess what happened during those days. Who knows what was won or lost? Perhaps the point never was *winning*, but rather the point was *dignity*.

"Following Jesus is not some nice little social event; it is a journey filled with struggle. If we want to follow Him, we have to be willing and ready to be bruised. After all, Jesus was *wounded*. Why should those of us who come after Him hope to live without being bruised?"

Up until this time, Cathy's suspicions of white people were buried deep. Of course, they go back to her childhood. But now she was facing them and the need for becoming reconciled to oneness. The Bible told her that, "There is neither Jew nor Greek, there is neither bond nor free, there is neither male nor female: for ye are all one in Christ Jesus" (Galatians 3:28).

Did she believe it and, if so, could she live it?

". . . be ye reconciled. . . ."

"The idea of all believers being one hasn't been an easy thing for me to accept, especially in regard to race. Racial reconciliation isn't easy for a lot of people. What makes the difference, however, is that I believe Scripture, and because I do, I have no choice but to accept this. What I did not always understand is that racial reconciliation had something to do with wholeness and this meant I had to face *my own* prejudices. And what I now understand better is that so much of our behavior is determined by how we *feel*. I learned that by acting upon what I *know* I could rid myself of these prejudices. (In this respect Ephesians 4:4–6 was especially helpful.)

"Through the years I have become friends with many dear white brothers and sisters. I think I've been helpful to them in understanding my race, and they've been helpful to me. Somewhere along my journey I came to terms with a very important truth: Jesus calls us to a new order. He requires us to live in a new dimension. I can be who I am because He really has reconciled me not only to Himself, but also to myself and to my world (2 Corinthians 5:17, 18)."

Now Cathy is a reconciler, bringing healing to others as well as to herself.

Some Canyons Are too Wide for Bridges

Upon graduation from Pepperdine, Cathy moved back to the South. She tried her wings at several different things, and then accepted a position as assistant dean of women at Mercer University in Macon, Georgia. The year was 1975.

If she thought her painful experiences were behind her, Cathy had another think coming. "Sometimes it seems as if some canyons are too wide for bridges. I pray I will have the courage to keep trying to build them anyway." She was confronted with another kind of suffering: loneliness!

Wanting to put her roots down, she sought out a place to worship on her first Sunday in Macon. She arrived at the church five minutes before the service, happy and humming a song. She was at peace and glad to be alive. The future looked bright and promising.

Five minutes later she was back in her car, where she burst into tears. She had been rudely met in the church and told that black people were not welcome at their services.

"There was nowhere to go and there was no one to talk to. I felt betrayed. . . . I just wanted to worship in God's house with His people."

But that morning as she tearfully drove to her lonely apartment, three very beautiful and graceful deer came out of the woods and crossed the road. As she stopped to let them pass, God spoke ever so gently to Cathy's heart: *There is still beauty in My creation.* She knew then that He was faithful and that He hadn't rejected her.

She also experienced alienation from blacks because of her education and position, which created another kind of problem. "I was suspected of being middle-class and not being 'black' enough to know what it was like to be poor, black, and emotionally unstable. A knife stab in the heart could not have hurt me more than this rejection by the people I wanted to love. Our roots were the same —how I longed for them to understand."

Cathy's quest for truth led her to the realization that *she* didn't really know herself who she was. "The day I admitted that, I began to be set free from the pain of alienation and loneliness that I'd been experiencing for so many years. God was then able to show me who I was as a human being, as His servant, as a black person. He was also able to show me who I was as a woman, as a single person, and as a professional. As I accepted who I was in Christ, my racial identity became less of an issue."

Waiting, Suffering, Rejoicing

Cathy still struggles with loneliness at times and there is one dream she harbors that hasn't come true. She is a typical woman. Her career has thrust her into the position where she does considerable speech-making and some travel is involved. "I go all over, giving of myself, and then I have to come home and be alone, and that is difficult and it hurts. But I also know that once you acknowledge where you are and you do what you can to change it, then there is nothing left to do but go on with your life. I am in the midst of going on with my life, sometimes with fear and trembling, and sometimes still with some anger, sometimes just with deep hurt and loneliness.

"Sometimes God asks us to wait. I wonder if having to wait wasn't one of the things Jesus suffered. Waiting is usually very painful for me. What I am beginning to understand more clearly is that when there is no apparent reason for waiting, we learn to be more patient with ourselves, with others, and with God. So I would have to say that no period of waiting for any of us is ever insignificant. Here's what I have learned: God makes us wait not just to show His power and greatness, but because He knows what is best for us."

Cathy likes to point others to Hannah Hurnard's powerful book *Hinds' Feet on High Places*. In that book the Shepherd tells the woman called Much-Afraid that Love and Pain go together. Cathy says, "Much-Afraid is surely one of my mentors. Just think, here was this person who was given Sorrow and Suffering as companions and told not to follow the Good Shepherd but she follows Him anyway. None of us really wish to suffer and we are very much akin to Much-Afraid.

"*Suffering has been the most creative force in my life.* As a black person, I used to think my ancestors had suffered so much that I shouldn't have to suffer. I thought I had suffered enough during my childhood so that I shouldn't have to experience it in my adult life. How wrong I was. I know now that suffering will last as long as I live, *but so will the joy.*"

II

Kathy Salerno

Love and Mercy Go a Long Way

"Do the best with what God has entrusted to you—don't measure yourself by others— leave the results with God."

There's a land where your dreams come true,
So far away yet so close to you.
Can you imagine what things you could do
In a land called love?

It's not a land of make-believe.
It's very real, and you can feel
Something you've never felt before—
The love of God and so much more. [1]

Those words from the award-winning musical production *The Music Machine* are much more than high-sounding phrases to Kathy Salerno, wife of the executive producer of that inspirational album. Actually, Kathy, as a young girl, harbored a dream. She wanted to go into the professional world of music as accompanist to a classical vocalist. She loved music. But *that* dream didn't quite come true; instead, she became the wife of Tony Salerno, founder and executive director of Agape Force. [2]

Agape = Love

Ask Kathy what *Agape Force* stands for and she'll reply, "Agape Force is just people who love God and are communicating this love in practical ways. *Agape* is a Greek word, really a Bible term that simply means 'love.' It's the kind of love that gives unselfishly without expecting anything in return."

Agape Force developed into an evangelical Christian missionary organization whose purpose has always been to prepare and mobilize people who can communicate this kind of agape love, as shown by Jesus Christ, to a lost and needy world—especially to those who may not be reached by traditional methods. And behind Agape Force, alongside her husband and a growing force of people motivated and bonded by love, has been Kathy, small of stature and slight of build, who has a heart of mercy.

Slowly, through the years, Agape Force has evolved into what it is today: a well-run, highly efficient organization whose methodology in approach and training stands up under the closest scrutiny. They learned through mistakes, many "firsts," and outreach efforts that preceded all that Agape Force is today.

The Love of God and So Much More

Music is *one* of the significant things that come into people's minds when they hear the name "Agape Force." For instance, in 1980, *Billboard Magazine* named *The Music Machine* as the Number One Inspirational Album of the Year. Obviously although the music and the musical production itself are especially appealing to children, they weren't the only ones responding—not with a rating like that!

Through the years there have been many musical productions, albums, and cassettes such as those done by the group called Candle and the Agape Force Prep School: *Nathaniel the Grublet, Bullfrogs & Butterflies,* and *Sir Oliver's Song,* in addition to Candle and the Agapeland Singers on *The Birthday Party* and *Lullabies* and now *Music Machine II.* Two other popular albums done by members of the Agape Force are: *To the Chief Musician* by Candle, and *Gingerbrook Fare* by Gingerbrook Fare. Silverwind, another music group from the Agape Force, has recorded *Silverwind* and *Song in the Night*. Kathy was one of the keyboard players in this group.

"My parents sacrificed to have me take piano lessons from the third grade on," she confides. "When I was only four years old and would get restless in church, I would pretend I was playing the piano by moving my fingers across the pews." That restlessness translated itself into a scholarship at the Southern California College of Music, where she met the young Italian who was destined to become her husband.

Tony was student body president and a very popular young man on campus. Kathy asked him out on a girl-asks-boy thing for their first date, a valentine party. It seems fitting that a couple who were to found a movement around the theme of love should begin their relationship on the day most commonly associated with thoughts of love.

Both Kathy and Tony were walking with the Lord, loving and serving Him, wanting to live out their lives in the most meaningful possible way. They didn't lose any time in either their commitment to Him or to each other—they were married in August 1966.

The Sky Is the Limit

"Tony had several different offers from churches in the southern California area to come and help with their youth programs. He was such a go-getter, of course they wanted him," she remembers with justifiable pride. Thus began a fast-paced, growing, two-and-a-half-year ministry in the little southern California church to which they felt God directing them. They had a very active coffeehouse ministry, one of the first in southern California in 1968, and a youth choir of a hundred which traveled around considerably. Tony directed and Kathy was the accompanist.

This was the late sixties, when a lot of things were happening—drugs were first coming on the scene and there was much rebellion and restlessness among young people. "God started stirring us to go beyond the four walls of the church," she relates.

A New Work

Kathy and Tony didn't know exactly what it was they were to do; they only felt a certainty in their hearts that they needed to raise up an army of people who loved God and would raise a standard to show the world what it means to be a Christian. They started with two young converts and soon realized they would need a larger place to stay.

A house became available through a Whittier, California, church in the spring of 1970. "The hippie movement was in full swing. People were burning down banks and buildings across the country and things were getting out of hand."

The Salernos welcomed these hippie kids into the big house and began ministering to their personal and spiritual needs. Kathy had a merciful heart that was always reaching out, helping others.

This is still the way the Agape Force ministry works—reaching out in one community after another, now all across the United States and Canada, as well as in other countries.

"One Way"

Back in the early seventies the "One Way" symbol became very popular. The Salernos helped popularize it. In July 1970 they held their first evangelistic concert in Los Angeles and called it the One Way Festival.

"By now we were using the One Way symbol," Kathy explains. "We had studied the work of William Booth and the Salvation Army, which had its start in England. That organization had a tremendous impact, literally changing some of the laws in England in the 1850s. It was a well-respected organization, and it was directed to the down-and-out person on the street. We found out that the One Way symbol came from that movement."

A Love Force

The Salernos went on to Santa Maria, California, which was Kathy's hometown. There they held their first citywide crusade and witnessed a tremendous move of God in that coastal community. Several people came out of that crusade to join their staff.

"Around that time we started talking about what we should call the work that we knew God was raising up. As we talked back and forth, we spoke often of a 'love force.' *Love* was a pertinent word among the hippies, as you may recall, but it was also a word that was so meaningful to us. Somehow we put together the name 'Agape Force,' and it was incorporated in the state of California in February 1971."

Breakthrough!

Reedley, California, was their first major breakthrough in this new outreach ministry. Easter week 1971 they went up with their team of workers to renovate a coffeehouse for a pastor in that community. The coffeehouse was completed—it was just a storefront in this small farming community, and it was called The Carpenter's Shop.

They were going to work, witness, and have nightly meetings for a week. That one week turned into thirteen! Revival broke out. The coffeehouse became the hub of excitement and the things that happened among the Mexican-American migrant workers resulted in television and other media coverage. The story was carried in several national magazines.

They had gone to Reedley with six full-time people. Now they were ready to leave with thirty-four people eager to go, wanting to train and get out to witness to others. "What do you do with *that* many people?" she asked.

Concentration Camp

Recognizing the need to properly train and equip these converts, the Salernos held a two-week intensive training school which they laughingly called Concentration Camp. Then they all went to work in an outreach in Oxnard, another coastal community, in an area known as The Colony.

Here is where their outreach ministry to children really began. "Children would come from far and near and the team workers were busy pulling puppet strings and putting on skits."

In August 1971 they opened their first Agape Force office in Fresno, California. "We had storefront offices and no money, but we prayed a lot! Our budget then—to provide housing, food, maintain offices and the coffeehouses, provide transportation, and meet the needs of all these people—was $13,000. God was very merciful, but we ate a lot of lettuce sandwiches too!"

The Salernos look back on those times as some of their best training. "We never went hungry and our needs were always met. It built character in all of us. The things we went through then are the backbone of this ministry."

Good News Spreads

Kathy and Tony were developing strengths that would better equip them to deal with the challenges that came their way. They recognized that their experience with the Lord was shallow at the outset of their work, so they spent much time in Bible study and agonizing in prayer.

While in Fresno, fifteen national students arrived from New Zealand as a result of their friendship with New Zealand evangelist Winkie Pratney and his high regard for what he saw God doing through them. This was a great encouragement to Kathy and Tony and was the beginning of what has since developed into annual international schools of intensive training. At the time they had no written materials, now, of course, they do. But they had classroom training along with out-on-the-street training—just learning to knock on doors, witness one on one in parks, on campuses, anywhere.

There was no stopping the Agape Force. Sometimes Kathy would step aside and try to appraise all that was happening. Like *The Music Machine* production said, she realized then—long before the song was written—that this wasn't "a land of make-believe."

Propelled by God's love and the burden each of them felt to reach the world for Christ, especially those who weren't going to churches, the work spread across the country.

Out Into the Fields

Kathy explains what a mission station is: "This is our permanent work in cities around the country, Canada, Mexico, and other foreign countries. We have many families and individuals who work out of these mission stations who keep their jobs and their homes, but who want to help in the work. They are what we call 'missioners.'

"There are some differences in the ministry now. We mainly started with single people; we've evolved from singles to marrieds, to marrieds with families, but there are still many singles too.

"Some of our workers were just young, raw recruits when they first became a part of the work, but they are up in their thirties now—we as an organization are not a child anymore, but coming of age in this ministry God has entrusted to all of us."

The Mother of the Ministry

Kathy has sometimes been called "the mother of the ministry." How does she feel about that? "I feel more like their big sister. When we started, I was twenty-five. I still think of us as eighteen-year-olds!"

Sometimes she starts comparing herself with others whom she admires who are also in ministry work, and she gets to feeling unsure about herself. "I have to talk with the Lord and wrestle it through. He's helped me see that I am to be myself, we all are, and we shouldn't measure ourselves by others. Do the best you can with what God has entrusted to you, and leave the results with Him."

Marriage and Ministry

Early in their married life Tony and Kathy learned that it is important to complement each other's personality with their own unique strengths. "I learned from him that being merciful doesn't mean excusing sin or unrighteousness, but understanding and helping."

Through these years of busyness and lots of travel, Kathy and Tony have managed to carve out a beautiful marriage relationship. How did they do it?

One of the things Kathy has done is to try to be Tony's ear in the ministry—listening to those who need help and attention. She tried to hear people out, identify with them, and help them herself. "This helps alleviate the load Tony carries," and it creates time and space for the Salernos to spend with each other.

Tony Salerno speaks of his wife with respect. "She has a gift of discernment and relies on the Holy Spirit to help her read countenances. We work well together. I've learned kindness, tenderness, and how to be merciful from my wife. We try to complement each other and work on building up the weaknesses, asking the Lord to help us develop strengths. You have to work at making marriage work, and we tell our couples this. Kathy works at it. When I travel, for instance, I know she will pack a little note for me to read. I like that."

Kathy says that you can't put more into your ministry than you do your relationship with each other. "There must be that balance," she emphasizes. "I've had to learn flexibility. I've really learned it best from my husband. We shouldn't be afraid to learn from our mates."

Growing Pains

In the early seventies, as the work grew, the Agape Force team began praying for a larger place, one that would be conducive to training more people. Their prayers were answered when the twenty-eight-acre estate owned by author-cartoonist Charles Schultz became available north of San Francisco up in the redwoods near Sebastopol. It was a dream-come-true type place, magnificently landscaped, with many buildings, a miniature golf course, a swimming pool, tennis courts, a four-hole golf course, riding stables, and a large recreation complex that was ideal for classrooms. "The Lord provided the finances and we moved," Kathy declares, still filled with awe as she remembers God's provision.

But after three years of working out of that part of the country, the Salernos realized how impractical it was to be so far removed from the rest of the nation. They needed to be more centralized. And they needed room for expansion and it was too expensive to build in California. Once again, God moved on their behalf, providing a lead on what has become their headquarters in the "Garden Valley" of east Texas. The California property was sold. The David Wilkersons were their neighbors; soon other ministries found property and prices in that part of the country to be ideal.

A visit to the Agape Force central headquarters is like stepping back into the old West. The outsides of the buildings have been made to appear rustic, but inside everything is up to snuff. The talent and creativity of the people is abundantly evident. "There are a lot of brainstorming sessions going on around here," Kathy laughs, "and we all work on various projects."

Inside one of the warehouse buildings, I saw props of every kind and description. "These are things we use in our musical productions. We have dancing trees and cabbages, fun things for our drama and musical groups to use."

There is a large and growing Christian prep school for staff children and also for children in the community.

There are orchards—apples, pears, peaches. And a large building where rabbits are raised for Third World countries. Perhaps you are wondering if there is anything that resembles a coffeehouse? Indeed, there is. It's called 'The Grublets' Hideaway.' There we sat eating popcorn and sipping one of "Nathaniel's Naturals," a delicious drink made with fresh fruit, blended together with all-natural ingredients, creating a thick and icy treat. The Hideaway is delightful with its old-time atmosphere. "The Grublets are actual characters from one of our albums," Kathy explained. "It's a word we coined for a little character. See them up in the balcony there?" and she pointed. There they were, peeking at us from their perch, just knee-high or so, cute little guys. "We have a whole drama presenting the Grublets."

But now there is space—lots of it—for growing, as the Lord continues to bring opportunities their way.

Let There Be Music

How has Agape Force survived? Where do the funds come from? This type of headquarters and work obviously cost lots of money. "In the early days of our ministry we had very little financial support coming in because we didn't feel we should ask help from others. We eventually realized that we were denying people the opportunity to share in the work by *not* making our needs known. However, we still survive to a large extent by doing now what we did at the outset."

While in Fresno, they recorded the first of what was to become many albums (eighteen at the time of this writing), several of which have become internationally known, earning some very highly prized awards in the music industry. They began selling their records door-to-door, and also the book *The Cross and the Switchblade.* "It struck home with us—to use books and music to raise funds for the work —a twofold service. We still get letters from all over, people telling us that the atmosphere in their home changed when their children began listening to the albums."

Kathy explained how their children's ministry evolved and how music has played such a significant role in their work. "Backyard drama and music emerged as effective tools for teaching youngsters about Christ in the early days. The result was the creation of the first children's album, *Agapeland,* and then a stage production to premiere the album. Day in and day out, as our teams roamed the streets witnessing, it was clear that children were suffering from neglect and abuse. It was heartbreaking. What child wouldn't respond to hopping cabbages and fun things like that?"

So began the birth of their musical productions and years of touring America, playing to standing-room-only crowds in churches, schools, civic auditoriums, and places like Knott's Berry Farm in southern California. *Agapeland* reached beyond anything ever imagined, but the Lord stimulated other projects that would even exceed that musical. Now several of their records and cassettes have been translated into other languages reaching millions around the world with the message of agape love.

The Music Machine is a musical production that created something like a human heart—if you put in good, good came out. When a verse from Galatians which names the fruit of the Holy Spirit was put into the machine, out came fantastic songs that generated interest and excitement about such themes as patience, self-control, gentleness, and love—character qualities which are so important in the development of children. It was fun and learning at the same time.

"Tony had a mandate from the Lord to start doing music already in 1972," Kathy relates. "So music has been a vital part of our ministry, a tool of evangelism, from the first." Of course music was

Kathy's forte, her big love, and it is a fair observation to make that without her dedication and expertise, the Agape Force music program would not be what it is today.

Parenthood Had to Wait

While Kathy's dreams of musical ministry were fulfilled early, her dream of being a mother had to wait. "We put off having children. It was a sacrifice for the ministry. We just didn't feel we had the necessary time that we knew it would take to devote to a family. But we did reach the point where we realized if we were going to have a family, we couldn't wait any longer. We were married sixteen years before little Anthony was born.

"I know it is a very popular thing now to have a child in your thirties. There are a lot of non-Christian philosophies circulating about this—women are putting off having their children because they want their careers. That's foremost to them, and they become accustomed to a certain life-style and like it. It was a big decision for me because I was content without a family, but somehow I couldn't imagine the rest of my life without children."

Kathy calls motherhood "a very special experience." She can't recall anyone ever telling her of the joys that come with having children. "What a mistake we make by not setting the record straight," she says. "I think as young women we see all the work and that when you have children you lose some of your privacy—those kinds of things—and we can lose our original desire to have children which, I believe, is a God-given natural thing for a woman. I look back now and wish someone had told me how exciting it is to have a child and to be a mother."

Kathy's life-style *did* change. Little Anthony Salerno arrived in September 1981. Tony and Kathy had never been separated for all the years of their marriage. So it was an adjustment. "I had always played for the musical groups and I've had to relinquish some of that. Yes, I miss being with Tony and having contact with others, but the baby and I still travel a little with him now and then."

Little Anthony was born with a hereditary condition called retinoschesis—a splitting of the retina. It is a rare affliction and medical science has no cure for it. Kathy and Tony won't know until the child can really communicate verbally with them how well he can see. "We are trusting the Lord for his eyesight and his future. We already feel there has been a change and even the doctors are marveling.

"God is seeking to prove Himself mighty to those who will pray and believe, and who will accept the challenges He places before them. Whether it is for our son's eyesight, and for other children we would like to have, or for the work of this ministry, Tony and I have determined in our hearts that we will trust the Lord and always be obediently responsive."

The lyrics of the song mentioned at the outset of this chapter come to mind. Can you imagine what things *you* could do in a land called love?

---

1. A LAND CALLED LOVE by Frank Hernandez and Sherry Saunders © Copyright 1977 Sparrow Song/Candle Company Music/World Artist Music Co., Inc. All Rights Reserved. Used by permission.

2. For more information on Agape Force, write P. O. Box 386, Lindale, TX 75771.

3. Candle is a team comprised of members of the Agape Force—singers and musicians who minister on the street, at schools, and in churches. Their goal is to communicate the love of Jesus Christ anywhere and by any means available to them. But Candle is much more than this; Candle is a visible witness of how Jesus Christ can change a life and cause it to shine in dark places. "No man, when he lights a candle, puts it in a secret place, but on a candlestick, that those who come in may see the light."

🌸 12 🌸

Edith Schaeffer

Personification of Graciousness and Continuity

"Our lives are statements—for better or for worse—revealing to those who follow after what we have lived and stood for, what has been most meaningful in our experience, and how successfully we have been able to instill that into the hearts of our children."

If tea and flowers stopped growing, and candles were no longer available, Edith Schaeffer would be sad, but not for long. Immediately her creative mind would be at work—a shell perhaps, a few leaves of ivy; depending on the place and what was available, she would gather them together, and even if it was only a glass of water, she'd invite you to sit down across from her, smile her warm, friendly smile, and extend her hands.

"Drinking something together, across a table like this, it gives a sense of togetherness, it makes a difference," she says. "If you were in my home—I don't care why you were there—I would have a teapot, cream, sugar, and at least two cups for the two of us, and a plate of I-don't-care-what. If I didn't have a live flower in the house, I would find the smallest pot of ivy and set it between us. Then you and I would experience a sense of togetherness."

Reading her books, you quickly recognize that graciousness has always been a part of her nature, that the gift of hospitality and the ability to extend herself to others in such warm and sensitive ways is as much a part of her makeup as her physical attributes.

She has an arresting face, framed by dark hair pulled back—sparkling brown eyes, the loveliest of smiles, and facial expressions that hold you captive when she talks. Her hands are just as expressive. She's small, vibrant, intense. She's been described as being a wife, mother, grandmother, author, speaker, hostess, and philosopher. And she does it all with unbridled creativity and enthusiasm.

In constant demand for years, both Edith and her husband, Dr. Francis Schaeffer, proclaimed by much of the media to be evangelicalism's most widely known scholar, speak at conferences, conduct seminars, lecture at universities, maintain L'Abri Fellowship in the Swiss Alps with branches in Holland, England, Sweden, and the United States, and continue to write books (his now number twenty-two, hers ten).[1]

Where does a work so widely known and so highly respected first get off the ground? And why? Why has this husband-and-wife team so captured the imagination and hearts of millions?

Edith Schaeffer, in answering those questions would direct your attention to the 650-page family autobiography, *The Tapestry*,[2] a monumental piece of work published in 1981.

Talking with Edith Schaeffer today, you cannot ignore her work in *The Tapestry*. She sees life as a tapestry.

Edith's Thread

Ancestors are an indisputable fact of life. Edith traces her paternal family lineage to Ireland, Scotland, and England. Recounting her family thread, and moved with emotion, she observes, "How can anyone be blasé about his or her existence?" Her pride is justified. Her father, George Hugh Seville, after hearing of the China Inland Mission and the need in China for the Gospel, sailed for the land and to the work that would claim his finest efforts and dedication.

Edith's maternal family lineage "covers a lot of history from a long line of Americans," she says as she traces it back to Revolutionary War days. Her mother, Jessie Maude Merritt Greene Seville, went to China as a young widow to become a missionary-teacher.

How do we come into possession of certain attributes which make up our personality? Edith's mother was stubborn; George was persistent. That, of course, doesn't sum up the totality of their makeup, but the man who was to become Edith's father fell in love with the little widow and diligently pursued her. The tenth time he asked Jessie Maude to marry him, she accepted. Several years later, Edith arrived on the scene.

Edith's father outlived her mother, and in reminiscing about her, he always spoke of his "talented, tactful, and true wife," and what a gracious woman she was, always so helpful to others. He felt that his daughters owed their mother a lot for their skills and for certain of their traits and characteristics. Edith underscores that it is important for us to realize that "our lives are statements—for better or for worse—revealing to those who follow after what we have lived and stood for, what has been most meaningful in our experience, and how successfully we have been able to instill that into the hearts of our children."

In looking at the progression of events and people in Edith's life, a word appears in her conversation that has become insolubly linked with her. The word: *continuity.*

Continuity

"Continuity is a part of who I am, and who you are. Recognizing something of what our ancestors had to suffer, as well as to enjoy, during their numbered years of life, is important in understanding what the human being that is me, or you, has to be or do. . . . We have something to do for the next generation too, something to pass on, something to start which they can go on with, something to prepare that they may complete. . . . We do not stand alone touching no one. We cannot slide into the water and cause no ripple. . . ."

This helps explain why the Schaeffers have become known for their interest in families—their own, of course, and the multiplied thousands of others whose lives have touched theirs through their ongoing, worldwide ministry both because of the work of L'Abri Fellowship, their writings, speaking, and, in more recent years, their film presentations.

Preserving a continuity in families—establishing and cherishing lasting family relationships, handing down from parent to child a knowledge of God's truth—these, Edith Schaeffer believes, are essential family priorities. Wherever she goes, whatever she writes, whatever she says—this thought is dominant. Through it all, Edith reveals herself as a parent: strong, loving, involved, excited about her four children and their mates, and her fifteen grandchildren not just because they are hers, but because she sees them as people in their own right who are diverse, productive, creative, and dedicated. Loving, ongoing attention to all the things that matter is at the heart of the Schaeffers' own lives. That continuity appeared threatened in 1978 when they learned at the Mayo Clinic in Rochester, Minnesota, that Dr. Schaeffer had cancer.

"I would say that the important thing is a basic attitude in life, whether it is toward marriage as a whole, or the difficulty of some unforeseen disaster hitting your home, or disappointment and change in your loved ones. There is, of course, a reaction when you first hear the word *polio* as we did with our son Franky in 1954 when he was two, or *cancer* as I did with my husband in 1978.

"I think it is a sad misuse of Romans 8:28 for people always to say that all things work together and that is it. You have heard of Pollyanna cheerfulness with this verse tacked on as your scriptural thing. We need to face whatever it is that confronts us, and we did face the news that my husband had cancer.

"Fran came down from the operating room and told me, 'It is malignant,' and we wept together for a few minutes. His first thought was that he wanted to call the children and tell them himself. My mind began working on what I could do to bring a togetherness there—a sense of continuity—and what we would do when we got back to the hotel. And we had to face the all-important question of treatment. Would we stay with the Mayo Clinic, or go elsewhere? So lots of things were flooding through my mind. As to handling it, I think that in the first minutes of handling a crisis there is a marshaling of the sort of thing one faces every day —how can I live through it? By doing one thing at a time."

Medical procedures were begun immediately in Rochester. God has kept Dr. Schaeffer active in a remarkable way, but the continuity of their life together called for adjustments and new patterns. Edith's husband bears the hard sentence of cancer in his body, but amazingly, it has not diminished the astonishing energy of his intellectual output.

"Now when we come back to the States three times annually for Fran's checkups, we come home," she says, explaining that once the decision was made for treatment to be received at Mayo she immediately began searching for a house. The children arrived from different parts of the world and they all worked together to bring this about. "It was a tiny little town house with dingy green walls, but we painted them white, got plants in, and made it a thing of beauty. How would you *do* a certain piece of creative work with this limit of time and space in a locality not necessarily of your own choosing, were it not something that was surrounded by a wall of circumstances that forced you into it?" she asks.

She answers her own question: "In the midst of a situation like that, there are some things that God will give you the strength to do. I couldn't go back to Switzerland and I couldn't go on with what I did at the chalet. I couldn't make a Sunday dinner for twenty-eight people. I couldn't write the next family letter. I couldn't do anything but take care of Fran at that time—but how could I do it so that it would be for his pleasure, joy, and ultimate well-being, and have it be a creative thing and ask God for strength to do it?"

An Important Basic Lesson

That kind of a mind-set was apparent in Edith already as a young woman, as Francis Schaeffer learned. They had met at a young people's meeting at the First Presbyterian Church of Germantown, Pennsylvania, in June 1932. They went their separate ways to college, communicating through letters and seeing each other on holidays and at vacation time, and then they married in July 1935.

" 'Till death do us part' is a big and important promise," she reflects, "and 'for better or for worse' is a fantastically realistic promise. A lot of time is being vowed, and a lot of situations are being suggested. This is a set of promises for imperfect people to make to imperfect people in an abnormal world where everything has been spoiled since the Fall! . . . "

She cautions about anyone being envious of the perfection they may mistakenly believe has existed in their lives. " . . . There are no perfect people, no perfect relationships, no perfect marriages. . . . There is no perfect formula for how to have perfection!"

The fact of imperfection surfaced almost immediately on their honeymoon trip. "The first thing we did after waving to the rice-throwing guests was to head toward the country and stop at a drugstore on the outskirts of town to cool off with a milk shake. In my elegant white suit, I sat on a high stool at the counter, sipping my chocolate milk shake; then when swirling around to get off, I found that someone else's milk shake had been spilled on the stool. My skirt was hopelessly stained with chocolate milk, ruined.

"Fran remembers clearly that he felt sorry, but that he felt the magic moment of starting out together was more important than the spoiled skirt. He also remembers that I had started to make a fuss about it, but that I stopped short and didn't mention it again. Stopped in midair, so to speak, I had made a decision that was *not* perfectly kept in our lives together, but which *was* made time after time. The decision was to stop, try to recognize the total value of what was happening, and make a deliberate choice that the broken, torn, spilled, crushed, burned, scratched, smashed, spoiled *thing* was not as important as the person, or the moment of history, or the memory."

The spoiled wedding suit was the first of countless times when she would be called upon to stop and make a deliberate choice about how she was going to react to a given situation. Her reaction would spell the difference between a host of chain reactions that could be set off among family members and/or those participating in the work of L'Abri Fellowship. No matter what the problem—money, sickness, major decisions about moving—she has applied this to her life. She can recall the many times, for instance, when they barely squeaked through.

Squeaking Through

Edith Schaeffer and her husband have always been able to sympathize with the many couples who have come their way who are squeaking through—just barely getting by while they are adjusting to life together. Edith, herself, became a working wife. "It seems to me that a woman's place is to share the life and the work of the man she has made a choice to say yes to, in whatever way the moment of history requires, with the possibilities and diversities being endless. The scope of going through life shoulder to shoulder in work, home, and vocation includes a variety of changing *roles*—if you want to use that word, which I don't like. So I did dressmaking, and I designed, made, and sold leather belts and buttons. The proceeds went to purchase our food and gas and so on—just enough to squeak through."

A daily pattern developed for the happy young couple as Fran started into seminary. "The challenge was to do it all on five dollars a week and keep it interesting. "My romantic ideas may have been a bit much, but looking back, that was preferable to not making any kind of attempt."

Edith is convinced of the value of trying to be creative, particularly because of how it affects children in the home. "A child will be affected by originality, beauty, and creativity. And a child in a Christian home should connect being in communication with the Creator God with having been made creative, in His image. Rather than creativity being squashed out, it should be enhanced and developed *because* of being brought up in a Christian home, not in spite of it." To that end, she would encourage turning off the TV, unplugging the Atari, and giving your children notepads and pencils, while urging them to try their hands at writing their own games and stories.

The Schaeffer children, and now the grandchildren, are evidence of a diversity of talent that was first noticed and encouraged when they were very young. "Don't wait until all the circumstances in your life are what you think they must be before you start being creative. We foolish mortals sometimes live through years of not realizing how short life is, and that TODAY is our life," she stresses. She would urge you to look for beauty where you are—in the unspectacular, the commonplace things of life. "You will be surprised. Stop dreaming!" Here is where her ideas about the importance of continuity really strike home. "Continuity is so important—to have familiar things around us wherever we are. Things that make us feel 'at home.'" The Schaeffers never travel without a fat candle, or a candlestick. For a couple who have spent the greater share of their lives in travel, living out of suitcases, you can begin to understand how important this becomes. Creating beauty wherever you are, and seeing God's handiwork, points to what Edith and Francis see as the central driving force of life—the Creator.

The Central and Most Important Continuity

Edith is quick to emphasize that continuity of familiar objects is not the central and most important continuity of the Christian life. "We are citizens of a heavenly country; we look forward to a home which is being prepared by God, which will be a creation of the all-perfect Creator, and which He has promised will be more marvelous and beautiful than we can possibly imagine. Of course we are willing to sacrifice in the area of material things as well as in all other areas, to put first the things of God. . . ."

Putting God first saw the Schaeffers in three parishes in this country before they sensed God calling them to go to Europe and minister to Protestant churches in Europe that were weakened by the devastation of war and the distressing influence of humanist theologians.[3] When they started packing their belongings, it was to go to an unknown place for an unknown length of time. By then they had three daughters—Priscilla, Susan, and Debby. "What is happening is a transfer of your children's childhood, and of family life from one side of the ocean to the other. As much continuity as possible needs to be packed into the trunks and boxes."

They had applied for a visa to live in Switzerland which they would use as a base for their travels throughout Europe for the next five years. Homesickness came in waves, but there were wonderful compensations such as the constant music of tinkling cowbells and the other country sounds and smells when they were "at home" in Switzerland. Even though their living quarters were unbelievably small, out came a tablecloth Edith's mother had embroidered and a pair of brass candlesticks. Continuity.

They responded to invitations from across Europe—Francis preaching and both he and Edith teaching.

Heidi's Switzerland

Dr. Schaeffer finally found a delightful chalet in Champéry, a village surrounded on all sides by towering alpine peaks. They felt this was really Heidi's Switzerland with the clarity of the air, the multitude of inviting paths waiting to be explored, and the peasant life which seemed to have gone on for a century unchanged.

Francis continued with his travels; Edith accompanied him when she could, and, at times, the children joined their parents. This was their introduction to the art, the culture, the music, and the grandeur of the magnificent buildings and history of Europe. But Edith's days for the most part were a busy mélange of caring for her daughters and a steady stream of girls who began coming to the chalet for tea and lively discussions, and in 1952 their son Francis August Schaeffer was born.

Champéry with its quaint charm had worked its way into the hearts of the Schaeffers. When the opportunity came for them to move into another beautiful and unusual chalet, at a low price, they made the decision to stay. It was this chalet that really became the starting point for the "question-and-answer" evenings with girls from finishing schools, and a host of other people.

Dr. Schaeffer was beginning to write articles, the embryo of books to be born many years later. Often people have asked Edith when her husband began to think the thoughts reflected in his writings. This was the context in which these things came into being. All of this was the development of a base for future work. The evening visits in their chalet with a growing number of people continued—a shadow of things to come unrecognized by the Schaeffers at the time.

Choices

The next several years were a time of searching, rethinking the whole matter of Christianity, with Dr. Schaeffer continuing in the work of strengthening the churches throughout Europe.

The Schaeffers have seen avalanches making their way down the mountainside with frightening rushes, sweeping everything away in their path. They became involved in battling the elements and watching helplessly as mud, stones, branches, and other debris came through the side windows of their chalet. But there was another kind of upheaval in their lives that came in 1955, calling for every ounce of strength and faith they possessed.

Dr. Schaeffer resigned from his mission board position in June of that year, the same month and year that L'Abri became a reality. Earlier that year Edith had written in the margin of her Bible the word *L'Abri*, which is French for "shelter."

"What were our visions or expectations or goals?" she asks. "Simply a desire to demonstrate the existence of God by our lives and our work. We asked, first, that God would help us answer honest questions with honest answers, that people might know of His existence in recognizing the truth of true truth; and second, that our living by prayer, and His answering in a diversity of areas, might also point lost people to His existence."

They were asking for "reality"; and they were to be overwhelmed by "reality"! "We wept, we laughed, we thrilled, we agonized, we squealed with surprise. Reality is not a flat plateau."

That was also the year they were given notice that they'd have to move from Champéry. At the time it seemed an incredible blow. "What *were* we going to do?" It became clear to them that what they couldn't do, God *could* do. Edith read Isaiah 30:17 and felt a bubbling song inside her that wouldn't be stilled. "This is my God who is *able* to bring us through affliction, dry our tears, and direct us clearly as to which way to turn."

Through a remarkable series of events orchestrated by the God of Elijah, Daniel, and Joseph—the God who specializes in doing the impossible—the Schaeffers found themselves moved into Chalet les

Mélezes in Huémoz, a charming village with a fabulous panorama of mountains.

The first month after Dr. Schaeffer's resignation people came from the United States, Holland, Germany, England, Canada, Greece, and Portugal. As time went on, as many as twelve countries would be represented at once—all of them sitting together in the Schaeffers' chalet, being graciously served by Edith. There were people of many different religious, or nonreligious, backgrounds. There were existentialists, humanists, liberal Jews, Roman Catholics, liberal Protestants, agnostics, and many other shades of thought represented. Some were very belligerent. Hour after hour, day after day, night after night, Fran could be found answering questions and leading discussions.

And where was Edith? If she wasn't at his side entering into the discussions, she would be in the kitchen, preparing a dinner for upwards of seventy-five people, or you might have found her coming from the fields laden with boughs and mountain flowers, full of ideas to decorate the chapel for an afternoon wedding, or she would be tending to the ongoing needs of her busy family. Always she managed somehow to keep in touch with people all over the world who wanted to be on their mailing list; or she would be writing, reading, praying.

Edith never neglected the training of her children; she always took time out to read to them. "I may have made the mistake of not taking enough days off, but that time of being alone with them in the evenings for reading, talking, personal questions, and togetherness at bedtime was precious, and protected from invasion!" She is big on urging parents to set aside such times with their children, and to work at building memories that will tie them together and last a lifetime.

The Realm of Ideas

In the years that followed, L'Abri expanded far beyond anything they had imagined. She explains their one rule regarding discussions as people from far and near gathered together: "Discussions for our own family and for those who joined us had to revolve around ideas and not organizations or personalities—that is, people. The realm of 'ideas' was a wide one, including art, music, books, creativity of a variety of kinds, science, philosophy, medicine, law, world events, religions, and how you can know the truth. Of course the Bible was read and discussed, but in a wide spectrum of being 'true' and 'important'—in the *whole* of life. Discussion was not categorized into subject matters and separated into 'disciplines' but invited thinking and recognizing relationships across the board."

As I sat with Edith Schaeffer at breakfast, sipping tea, we shared ideas about how she sees life today. How do we break out of the so-called "Christian ghetto" where so much of our thinking and our conversation is often just a mouthing of phrases? "By being convinced that what we have is truth and not just 'religious'; and by not being afraid to face the questions themselves and then to face other people's questions."

Sometimes as Christians we say one thing but then our actions in life are totally different. "Where is the fear of the Lord?" she asked. "Where is the recognition that sin is really sinful, where is the real awe, the real remorse and repentance?

"I often pray in our little Swiss chapel, 'Lord, make us solid oak. Don't let us be veneer. Don't let us be plated silver. Don't let me be just a surface thing.' "

If there is one thing that differentiates a L'Abri conference from others, Edith feels it is their insistence that "All of life is spiritual. People say this is spiritual—reading my Bible, reciting prayers, putting hands up in praise, or whatever—the rest of their lives is lived in neutral." This dichotomy is a source of concern to her.

"We teach strongly that if God would have you write music or paint, play the violin, or perform in some way—whatever—that this is just as spiritual. If you are creating that which He has made you to be able to create and do, then you are exhibiting the wonder of God's creation and that is a spiritual act. . . . What you have got to weigh is *what truth is*. The reason so many do not have real answers to the questions the world asks is that they are not sure of the answers themselves."

A Genuineness in Being

We talked of her family. One by one the Schaeffer children married and established homes of their own.[4] Then the grandchildren started arriving. Such joy! Ask her what a family is[5] and she replies: "A formation center for human relationships—worth fighting for . . . worth the dignity of hard work."

To get to know Edith Schaeffer is to come to love the genuineness of her being. And it is to sense a deep family loyalty—not just for her own immediate family members, but for the larger family of God of whom God is our Father.

"None of us as family is a finished product like a Rembrandt hanging in the museum, or a piece of Bach that doesn't change. We aren't finished, we are changing and we are shifting generations gradually.

"Death doesn't break the family, nor does death put a hole or a tear in The Tapestry. We as threads are important for the time we've been woven in, during our present history, and we have had significance in affecting past history. We know nothing of the future, but whether we are to be here long, or whether we are to go to be in heaven earlier than anyone expects, we will be affecting future history. . . . But one thing we know, whether the 'ending' of our thread in the pattern is sooner or later, we approach a new beginning, and not an ending. Our new beginning is a promise made by the true Living God who never breaks His promises."

---

1. *L'Abri, Hidden Art, Christianity Is Jewish, What Is a Family? A Way of Seeing, Affliction, Everyone Can Know* (with Francis Schaeffer), *The Tapestry, Lifelines,* and *Common Sense Christian Living.*

2. Edith Schaeffer, *The Tapestry* (Waco, TX.: Word Books, 1981). Material excerpted in this chapter used by permission of the publisher.

3. Dr. Schaeffer had been asked by the commission of the Independent Board and the men of the American Council of Christian Churches to go to Europe.

4. Oldest daughter, Priscilla, with husband, John Sandi, are at Swiss L'Abri.

They have one married daughter, Becky. Second daughter, Susan, and her husband, Ranald Macauley, are in charge of the Greatham branch of L'Abri in England. They are parents of four children. Youngest daughter, Debby, and husband, Udo Middleman, are also at Swiss L'Abri. They, too, have four children. Franky, the youngest of the Schaeffer children, lives with his wife, Genie, and three children in New England. Franky is the only one of the children not directly working in L'Abri, Edith noted, but he is a filmmaker working to put his father's ideas out into the world, a writer (two books out, third on the way), and a speaker in his own areas of the present-day "battles."

5. Edith has a book entitled *What Is a Family?* published by the Fleming H. Revell Company in which these ideas are more fully amplified.

Cory SerVaas

Making Journalism a Healing Profession

"I have promised God that I would work every day, for the rest of my life, to help in the prevention of cancer."

She walks briskly. When you are not accustomed to walking *that* briskly, you sort of have to run just to keep up with this busy and energetic lady. When Cory SerVaas isn't walking briskly, she's working feverishly at her desk. For her, it isn't a feverish pace—whether walking or working—it's normal. How else could she possibly get everything done? How else could you explain the multifaceted career this unusual woman has had since she was a young woman just out of school?

Today she reigns as editor and publisher of the venerable *Saturday Evening Post,* an accomplishment that ranks her among many notable predecessors, including Benjamin Franklin. But none of these worthies were women. If that were her only claim to fame, it would be impressive enough, but Cory SerVaas is also a medical doctor, a devoted wife, and the mother of five children.

Dr. SerVaas fills all her roles with the same drive and energy, but she has focused her life's work in a combination of publishing and medicine. One of her key concerns is the battle against cancer.

"I really have a burden on my shoulders," she explains. "I feel as if I have to help find the reason why we see so much cancer in the world today. I probably can't accomplish this in my lifetime, but if I can just help inch the research along a little bit, prodding here and there, I will feel I have helped to make a contribution in this battle."

That of course helps to explain the indefatigable drive of Cory SerVaas. But it is not just cancer research that has captured her interest. She authors regular medical feature columns and a column, "Medical Mailbox," which appears in the *Post*. These writings reflect the broad range of her interest, aimed at informing the public —topics range from malignant melanoma, to herpes, to the effects of cigarette smoking and drinking of alcoholic beverages on the pregnant woman, to arthritis and gallstone research.

She speaks of all that is already known in the field of medicine that must be conveyed to the public. "We must educate more people about these things," she says with a note of urgency in her voice. This zest for educating the public led to the publication of two monthly newsletters: *Cancer Prevention* and *Medical Update*. [1]

"I have a tremendous sense of urgency now to be more creative. Not only must we do all we can to prevent cancer, but we must use technology to speed us along." Talking rapidly as she walks briskly down the hall to a large room where computers are tabulating results of the *Saturday Evening Post* health surveys[2] (Help Prevent Cancer Survey, Help Prevent Heart Attacks Survey, Lessen Your Cancer Risk Survey), she exudes grateful enthusiasm for this marvel of a machine which is speeding up the process of providing medical research data.

She Knows How to Salvage the Minutes

Her energy and desire to get things done now have earned for her the reputation of being a demanding boss—something she doesn't deny. "That's why I keep two shifts—day and night—of secretaries going. I do work hard because I enjoy what I'm doing. I expect a lot from myself and I expect a lot from others. We try to attract people who feel a lot of enthusiasm for what they sense we are trying to do.

"Time management is to do three things at once whenever possible." She laughs as she says it, but you sense she's become an expert at that kind of juggling. "I try not to do anything that does not require my services, so I'm not the typical homemaker in that I try not to wash dishes or do the shopping. I delegate the housework and the less important details of my life."

When Cory was going to medical school, she and her children studied alongside each other. "They helped *me* study," she insists, adding, "I didn't do their homework for them. We taught our kids to take responsibility for their lives very early. All children need to develop self-sufficiency, and I'm glad I can truthfully say ours did learn this."

She is a firm believer that less mothering and more teaching children to be resourceful by setting a good example is vital. "I would never discourage any career-minded woman from having a family, because I think children learn so much more by example. If you're sitting there yourself studying or doing something constructive, I think the likelihood of your children veering almost naturally in that same direction is very good.

"When my husband and I were going to medical school, we had a large chalkboard in our bedroom, and we had, in effect, our own school. The children learned all the cranial nerves right along with us. They learned a lot about medicine."

Today, two of the SerVaas children are lawyers, two went to Harvard, and another son is working in the preventive health field. Cory is proud of her family, and well she should be, but she's also very modest, preferring to give most of the credit to her husband. "Having a father participate in the day-to-day activities of your children, in addition to the mother, makes sense to me," she explained. "And our children had a marvelous father. He did a lot of fathering. We've had a lot of family togetherness—we've worked hard and we've played hard *together*. And we do play. We play tennis, we ski, we swim laps in the summertime, and we exercise to keep in good physical condition."

Both Cory and her husband rise early and work late. They each have an office in their home as well as at their jobs. There are libraries and phones in every room of the house, and a typewriter in the kitchen and one in their bedroom. "If we get an urge to do some creative writing, we can just run on over to one of the typewriters," she commented. "I do a lot of early-morning writing, often writing an article before I go to work. By getting up at 4:30 A.M., I can write in peace undisturbed."

Benjamin Franklin would have approved of Cory's regard for the wise use of time. Among his many sayings are these: "Up, sluggard, and waste not life; in the Grave will be sleeping enough." And, "Lose no time. Be always employed in something useful. Cut off all unnecessary actions."

"There Was a Child Went Forth"

Where did Cory SerVaas get her no-nonsense approach to life? Walt Whitman wrote poetic lines speaking of the child going forth every day, and the first object he looked upon, that object he became, showing the influence upon the child of the home and his cultural environment. A glance backward at Cory's childhood provides some clues as to the woman she is today.

She was one of four children born on a farm near Pella, Iowa, a bastion of Reformed theology. Cory grew up on daily Bible reading at the table after every meal, and it was the custom for prayers to be prayed before the meal, invoking God's blessing on the food, and afterward thanking Him for His daily provisions. It was a strict upbringing, with little foolishness allowed. The children learned very early in life about the virtue of the work ethic, and there was always plenty of work to do on the farm. Cory speaks proudly of her Dutch ancestors. "My great-grandfather was one of the early pioneers and founders of the first Dutch Reformed Church west of the Mississippi. He was among a group of people who were highly motivated to make things better for themselves and others. They came from Holland in 1846 and suffered a lot of deprivation and hardships. I think I have that spirit in my blood."

Cory's mother, Gertrude Dendurent, underscored the validity of her daughter's remark. "Cory has always had that driving force," she stated. "She started school when she was four."

"It was a country-school education," Cory chimed in.

"She was always looking after her younger brother and other children," her mother recalled. "She showed a talent for writing very early in life, and she also had a talent for drama—she would be in all the skits and school plays. She was very active, and always reading. She never did have time for dishes. . . ." Mother and daughter laughed. We were visiting with her mother who, at the time, was in an Indianapolis hospital, recovering from surgery and showing the same spunk that characterizes her daughter.

"I've never stopped reading," Cory admitted. "I read everything in sight—every sign on billboards—you know, that kind of thing. If it's in print, I want to know what it says."

The thing that stands out from her childhood is the old missionary who walked ten miles to the schoolhouse every Thursday afternoon come rain or shine. "This little old man with a beard looked like something right out of the Bible. He came to teach the Bible and he would bring his little dog-eared lesson books. I remember how he would have us memorize verses from the Bible and the catechism. I think about that when they talk about taking prayer and religion out of our schools. He didn't come just to our school, he made the rounds to other schools on different days. He wasn't paid to do this, he simply went to teach little children about the love of Jesus. He lived to be a very old man; he had such faith. This man had a great influence upon my young life. In later years I often reflected upon him and his faith."

An Inventive Mind

Upon completion of high school, Cory went to the University of Iowa and graduated from their School of Journalism in 1946. She went on to do postgraduate work at Columbia University in New York City to work on a master's degree in journalism. "I did all the Columbia work part-time, at night school. During the day I was editor at Lionel and wrote a booklet on chemistry experiments for kiddies."

She was in her early twenties, and her creative mind was hard at work. She invented the patented apron hoop, a device used for the production of aprons—it curves around the waist, making apron ties unnecessary.

Right about this time, when she could use the help of a male, a tall, dark-haired, handsome man crossed her path and, she'll tell you today, "It was love at first sight." She met Beurt SerVaas at a New York City church. The name Beurt rhymes with flirt and, at first, Cory thought he was coming on a bit strong. "He was there with his beautiful sister, and I thought they were man and wife. He acted so interested in me and I couldn't understand it until his sister took off her gloves and I noticed she wasn't wearing a wedding band. Then my response to him changed! But it took me two years to get him to the wedding. We were engaged in 1949 and married in 1950 and had five children in seven years!"

Beurt SerVaas offered his services to help her in whatever way he could with her booming apron hoop business. Of course Cory welcomed the offer. After they were married, the venture was so successful that, in her words, they were "financially independent." They felt it was a very special gift from the Lord, and it has been an ongoing, successful patent for them.

"I thank God daily for the wonderful, good things He has brought into our lives. That invention made it possible for us to buy our big house on twenty-five acres in Indianapolis where we could raise our family. Little did we know that in time it would enable us to be only seven minutes from the great medical center where we both went to study medicine."

She Wanted Her Life to Count

In pursuing medicine, Cory was fulfilling a lifelong interest that had lain dormant for many years. "I wanted my life to count; I really wanted to do something that would be considered truly worthwhile. A relative in Iowa was a surgeon and people would tell me how he saved their lives. I think I grew up thinking that that was one of the *really* important things you could do with your life.

"I never dreamed that the day would come when I could actually go to medical school, that I could take the time to go back to college and still keep our homelife going and care for the family. But suddenly everything became possible because of having financial independence as a result of the apron hoop invention. So I was able to start premed school right after our youngest daughter, Amy, started kindergarten. I started out part-time and then worked up to full-time."

Beurt SerVaas had a manufacturing business going at that time. His father had been a sales executive with Uni-Royal and many years later Beurt would buy the business, renaming it the Indianapolis Rubber Company. The SerVaas business ventures expanded into many areas which would, in time, include purchasing majority interest in the Curtis Publishing Company stock and reviving the *Saturday Evening Post.*

When his energetic wife went to med school, Beurt SerVaas decided to go back to school too. She graduated in 1969 as a medical doctor, and he graduated in 1971 with a Ph.D. in medical science. "The same courses, except the clinical," she explains.

Does she have an active patient practice? The answer to that is actually yes and no. Medical publishing is her primary practice. Her husband says, "Can you imagine such a quirk of fate—she got a medical degree after she got married, and she got a magazine to go along with it!" Quickly they both react. They know it wasn't just "a quirk of fate," but it was the hand of God. The SerVaases were being prepared for their utmost challenge—that of blending the field of medicine with publishing.

Theirs is an active Christian faith, a strong belief in and reliance on the providence of God. When they acquired the *Post,* according to their religion editor, Bob Silvers, "Cory was very supportive of my efforts to put Christian articles in the magazine, and was also very active herself in making suggestions along these lines. She believes in the magazine's championing a Christian perspective throughout its pages. She subscribes to the philosophy that spiritual health is as important as physical health. So the two subjects make up a good portion of the magazine's editorial content."

A Different Kind of Patient

Although she serves as company physician for the several SerVaas manufacturing companies and refers patients, and performs routine screenings for Curtis Publishing employees, through her prolific publications interests she is most effectively spreading the gospel of preventive medicine. In this way she has been able to make journalism a tool of medicine. Interestingly enough, she has much in common with the founder of the *Saturday Evening Post* himself, who was a crusader for preventive medicine in his own right.

The *Post* was Benjamin Franklin's brainchild, conceived as the *Pennsylvania Gazette* in 1728, when there were only five regularly published newspapers in all the colonies, all local in scope. The history of the *Post* is fascinating, encompassing more than two hundred fifty-five years.

When the *Saturday Evening Post* folded in 1969, a shocked world gasped that this could happen to what had become the best-known magazine in publishing history. At the time, circulation stood at seven million. It was unthinkable that the magazine that grew up with America and helped the nation smile through countless troubled times now had fallen on hard times, weakened, unable to carry on. It was like having to part with apple pie, patriotism, and the Fourth of July. Actually, for the Curtis Publishing Company, it was a combination of several things, including bad business judgment, a turnover in top management, and rising postal rates. Who could revive this fallen empire?

After twenty months of *Post* dormancy, Beurt and Cory, who were already publishing *Child Life* magazine, became interested in buying *Jack and Jill*, another well-known children's magazine, from the near-defunct publisher in Philadelphia. But when the attorneys working on the bankruptcy case observed the SerVaases' interest, Beurt and Cory were approached to take over the entire operation.

It was a challenge they could not pass up. So in 1971, the Doctors SerVaas had an ailing magazine on their hands that desperately needed reviving. One of the first things they did was move the "patient" to their headquarters in Indianapolis. The *Post* then went into what Cory calls "intensive care" for some months.

"Getting the *Post* was so tremendous," she says with obvious delight and what could be described as an almost little-girl awe that this marvelous good fortune should have come their way.

The New *Saturday Evening Post*

Norman Rockwell, the revered American illustrator, whose name and career were synonymous with the *Saturday Evening Post*, became acquainted with the SerVaases and casually revealed to a television audience that he understood the magazine was to be reborn. People responded with gratitude.

"The *Post* was so revered in the hearts of the American people that some told us they cried tears of joy when we brought it back into existence." So it was that in 1971 the *Saturday Evening Post* once again hit the newsstands and the circulation soared.

"The *Post* has always had so much credibility, it's always been so believable, that we knew we had *the tool* to disseminate medical information and the things we are constantly learning as a result of our reading and research. We wanted to retain the emphasis on its being a family publication and put optimism and wholeness along with the much-loved *Post* cartoons and humor into each issue. It has dovetailed and fits so beautifully with our interests—just think how many people read each issue!"

Readership studies show that the *Post* has an audience of 5 million readers per issue because of the large pass-along readership figure.

It can be said that a valuable continuity in American life was restored with the new *Post*. Not only did the SerVaases take over the *Saturday Evening Post*, but in 1976 Cory founded the Benjamin Franklin Literary and Medical Society, Inc., a nonprofit educational organization of which she is chairman. In 1980 this foundation purchased several well-known children's magazines. "Good health can be taught," she insists, "and instruction should begin with the very young and continue throughout life. To change society, you have to start with the kids, get them to eat right." These children's magazines, numbering nine in all[3] aim at doing that.

"We also publish *The Health Connection*, which is a monthly newsletter for parents.[4] We have one goal in mind: insuring the happiest, healthiest infants and children possible," she affirms.

The 700 Club Saves Baby's Life

In October 1982, Cory and the *Post* became involved in a weekly TV program entitled "Lifecare Digest,"[5] with the popular "700 Club." The program is taped at the *Post* headquarters in Indianapolis and is hosted by Cory, who discusses what is new in medicine, nutrition, and personal health care.

She tells of a young flight attendant, Susan Norman, flying with Eastern Airlines, who had watched a demonstration of infant CPR (cardiopulmonary resuscitation) on the program, just hours before a flight from Seattle to St. Louis. Susan was able to put into practice what she had seen, thus saving a child's life.

"Of course this is what it's all about," Cory states.

Cory's Hard-hitting Columns Get Results Too

She is especially gratified when she receives letters from viewers of the TV program, and from readers of her monthly columns and the newsletters telling of their experiences as a result of something she's brought to their attention. She tells of one man who wrote from his hospital bed as he recuperated from surgical removal of a malignant melanoma. He'd seen a photo in the "Medical Mailbox" column in the *Post*, and upon comparing it to his mole, properly identified his own malignancy early.

A subject of special interest to her is the importance of fiber in the diet. In fact, so convinced was she of the link between a number of degenerative diseases and the fiber-depleted diets common in modern societies today, that in 1978 she collaborated on a cookbook designed to incorporate more bran and fiber in the diet.[6] Research on that subject took her to the Republic of South Africa to meet with Dr. Alexander R. P. Walker and to the Caribbean to meet with Dr. Denis Burkitt. Both men are credited with alerting the health-care industry to the need for high-fiber diets (high in grains and vegetables, low in fats and refined sugars) as a means of reducing the risk of cancer in the colon and elsewhere.

Another topic of great concern to her is the effects of the amino acid lysine on persons suffering from herpes-type viruses.[7] "The bottom line is that we're trying to fit some pieces of the jigsaw together," she emphasizes, explaining that the theory that lysine might lessen the incidence of some kinds of cancer is based on recent research findings and the *Post* health surveys.

"We Can Make These Times Better"

In two years' time, Cory saw three family members restored to health after experiencing severe health problems, any one of which might have claimed their lives. She credits their recovery and the fact that they are alive today, first of all, to the Lord's goodness and in answer to their prayers and the prayers of others; and then to the fact that they, as a family, do practice preventive-health measures and they are informed.

"These experiences have greatly strengthened my faith," she humbly acknowledges. "I would have to say they have been the most significant turning point in my life with the Lord. Since then I have promised Him that I would work every day, for the rest of my life, to help in the prevention of cancer. I have great impatience to get everything done before the final curtain falls."

It is undeniably true that as a nation we are overindulgent, relying upon the doctor with a magic bullet rather than taking the responsibility upon ourselves to stay well. "I would like to see people start with the reflection that good health, the very rudder of our life journey, is not a right, but a job it is up to each of us to perform. Your health is a great treasure to be guarded.

"It takes a long time to get sick and once you are sick, the doctor isn't a magician and often can't reverse something that took years to develop. But remember, it is never too late to take care of your health. In my writings, I address this in hopes of inciting interest. Reformers are not popular, so I just have to keep repeating my message over and over again, sandwiching it between postscripts and fiction."

What she was saying sounded familiar, only she was saying it somewhat differently. As you leave the *Saturday Evening Post* offices, you walk past a big board room with a massive table and chairs. I glanced at the wall with its shelves containing current copies of just about every known magazine. Above this I read: WE CAN MAKE THESE TIMES BETTER IF WE BESTIR OURSELVES. It was signed, Benjamin Franklin.

"Let's go!" There she was walking briskly out of her office. I fell in step alongside this dynamo of a little woman called Cory. She was off to do some more "bestirring" in the hope that others would do the same.

---

1. *Cancer Prevention* and *Medical Update* are published monthly by the Medical Education and Research Foundation, a division of the Benjamin Franklin Literary & Medical Society, Inc., a nonprofit organization, at 1100 Waterway Blvd., Indianapolis, IN 46202. They are available by subscription and membership in the foundation and a contribution of $12 or more with an annual membership.

In January 1982, the Curtis Publishing Company sold the *Saturday Evening Post* to The Saturday Evening Post Society, a division of the Benjamin Franklin Literary & Medical Society—a move designed to help the *Post* expand its efforts into the area of preventive medical research.

2. Participation in these surveys is welcomed and, in fact, urged. Write to the address listed above and ask for copies of all their health surveys.

3. The children's magazines can be ordered by name from the subscription office at: P. O. Box 6500, Bergenfield, NJ 07621. Write and ask for information and subscription price for: *Child Life, Jack and Jill, Humpty Dumpty, Children's Digest, Turtle Magazine for Preschool Kids, Children's Playmate, Health Explorer, Medical Detective,* and *Junior Medical Detective.*

4. *The Children's Health Connection* monthly newsletter is published by the Children's Better Health Institute, a division of the Benjamin Franklin Literary & Medical Society, Inc., and can be ordered at the address given above for a contribution of $15 or more with an annual membership in the foundation.

5. Watch your local TV guide for channel listing and time of program in your area.

6. *The Saturday Evening Post Fiber & Bran Better Health Cookbook* is published by the Curtis Publishing Company (1977), 1100 Waterway Blvd., Indianapolis, Indiana 46202.

7. The herpes-type viruses include chicken pox, mononucleosis, shingles, Bell's palsy, Ménière's disease, and the more common facial and genital herpes. It now appears there may be a correlation between the dietary habits of people with Burkitt's lymphoma, a viral cancer, and a high-arginine, low-lysine diet. Foods that should be omitted to achieve a high lysine-to-arginine ratio include chocolate, peanut butter, peanuts, and gelatin, among others. Arginine and lysine are amino acids found in protein foods. The *Post*, in its health surveys, is asking readers: Do you know families who have had combinations of Burkitt's lymphoma and a herpes-type virus?

Many people have found that, by eating a low-arginine diet along with taking the food supplement lysine, they can prevent herpes recurrences. The *Post* findings are sufficiently exciting to make Dr. SerVaas want to get other surveys in in order to check the hypothesis: Does lysine decrease the incidence of cervical cancer? and if that form of cancer, what about other cancers?

Rexella Van Impe
A Lady With a Tender Touch

"It is hard to be a childless woman when you have the heart of a mother. . . . But what could be better than having children? Only having God's will."

It's enough to make even the most seasoned interviewer nervous. Television lights are glaring, cables and equipment are strung everywhere. Cameramen are zooming in as they call out to each other in their trade jargon; the men in the control booth are peering intently at the monitors; someone from the makeup department rushes up with a powder puff, "You're shiny, right *there*," and she gives a quick pat on the guest's forehead— organized confusion it might appear to an outsider. But Rexella Van Impe, television talk-show hostess, takes it all in stride, putting her guests at ease, laughing with them, complimenting them on how nice they look, thanking them once again for accepting the invitation to appear on the program ("Jack Van Impe Presents"). She reaches out, touching her guest's hand ever so slightly. "It's going to be a *good* interview."

In the weeks to come, viewers all across North America will respond to that interview. The *Chicago Tribune, Miami Herald,* and *Atlanta Journal* have all reported the meteoric rise of the program. Millions watch annually. That's a lot of people. And Rexella senses it. Hers is a responsibility not taken lightly.

Guests are chosen from a diversity of backgrounds—there are businessmen and -women, politicians, lawyers, doctors, educators, psychiatrists, military men, theologians—and interviews may be on location someplace in Hawaii or Alaska, or London, Jerusalem, Rome, Toronto, Dallas, Nashville, or Washington, D.C. For instance, Rexella interviewed Glenn Hester, a man raised in foster homes, and much abused as a child. Glenn's book, *Child of Rage*, told his readers of the rage that almost destroyed him. In interviewing him, Rexella said, "You've given readers something that deeply disturbs my heart. As I read the book sometimes I was angry, but much of the time I was filled with fear for other children who are going through the same crises that you experienced."

Hester was one of many Rexella has talked to regarding childhood memories. Perhaps she has a deep interest in asking people about their backgrounds since her own happy childhood stands in such contrast to the childhood of so many of her guests. The middle child in a family of three children, Rexella was the dainty and adored only daughter of Rex and Esther Shelton.

"Ours was a very secure and peaceful home that reflected the touch of gentle, godly parents." She speaks of her mother's soft-spoken ways—a woman with boundless energy; and of her father's jovial and discerning disposition—a man who wasn't afraid to say and to show to his children that he loved them.

Now, all little girls want to grow up to be beautiful, and Rexella was no exception. When she was just a little girl, she complained to her mother about the way she looked. Her very wise mother took her daughter to 1 Peter 3:3, 4, which speaks of the way one looks, and emphasizes the importance of the inner spirit ". . . which is in the sight of God of great price."

Rexella never forgot the lesson, but she needn't have worried. Today, the beautiful hostess of the weekly television program "Jack Van Impe Presents" has become known and admired not only for her beauty and charm, but for a gracious inner spirit which reflects, in a meekness and quietness, a sincerity that viewers recognize as being genuine.

The Lady in Red

It was this combination of beauty and gentle spirit that first caught the attention of young Jack Van Impe, billed by the Pontiac Youth for Christ organization as "Jack Van Impe, Accordionist Supreme." It was at a rally in this Michigan city that the two first met.

Rexella, dressed in a red suit with a small white ermine collar, stepped on stage to sing, and the accordionist did a double take. When she sang and then explained in her testimony that she felt God was calling her to some work in evangelism, his heart melted. When she turned to go back to her place, their eyes met. Now it was her turn to notice—and notice she did! He was dark and handsome. When he smiled his deeply tanned face seemed to light up and his eyes crinkled pleasantly at the corners. It was a case of mutual love at first sight.

Their courtship progressed largely by mail, with Rexella away at college and Jack involved in evangelism work. But her admiration for him grew as she sensed the depth of his commitment to the Lord, and on August 21, 1952, they were married.

Marriage to a Traveling Evangelist

The newlyweds had planned to spend their honeymoon at Mackinac Island, a beautiful resort near the straits of Mackinac, in Michigan. But the first night of their trip, they stopped at a Bible conference in Traverse City, a picturesque place on the shore of Lake Michigan. "Jack was to speak at a Saturday night youth rally, but they prevailed upon us to stay another day, then another. We spent our entire honeymoon at the Bible conference," she laughingly recalls. "We never did make it to the island; but we had a wonderful time of playing, singing, and speaking at the services."

For the next twenty-eight years of their marriage, at times it seemed to the two of them that all they did was live out of suitcases. Much in demand, seldom were they home. The honeymoon gave a preview of what their life together would be, but as Rexella's husband quips today, "The honeymoon has continued."

Rexella was strong encouragement to her husband, who had applied himself with diligence to a program of Bible memorization that was to earn for him the title The Walking Bible.

Jack's sermons, delivered without notes, and Rexella's music made them a combination that captured the hearts of audiences in city after city. His manner of delivery was fiery—an evangelistic approach that demanded attention and produced results. Rexella, on the other hand, was tender but strong, soft-spoken, pleasant to look at and listen to. They demanded excellence of themselves, yet without yielding to professionalism, and they were human and happy enough for people to accept them warmly. Early in their ministry they adopted a format that the crowds genuinely appreciated.

"Women by the thousands have told me they appreciate the love Jack and I show toward each other. When introducing him, I would relate a humorous incident we had experienced, and then Jack would get back at me. He always enjoyed ribbing me about being a southerner."

Jack enjoyed teasing his wife on or off the platform. "When I first met Rexella," he'd tell audiences, "I had to teach her to wear shoes to revival meetings. I filled them with sand for two years so she would feel at home."

Rexella rightly concluded after several years of marriage that the path her husband had chosen to follow would continue to require rigid self-discipline not only for himself, but also for her. Her fragile body found the traveling draining. She soon found that she had physical problems that proved to be more than just a thorn in the flesh. Sometimes she would collapse with fatigue and pain after ministering for hours on end alongside her husband on the platform. They may have kidded good-naturedly during the programs and services, but for Rexella it was definitely not all fun and games. A fine gynecologist correctly diagnosed the cause of her problems and strongly recommended a hysterectomy. Since that would have eliminated the possibility of having children, Rexella was determined not to have the operation.

"That decision almost cost me my life," she admits today.

Pain: A Way of Life

In her book, *The Tender Touch*, [1] she acknowledges that her "thorn in the flesh" for those many long years was her health.

"Through illness Satan tried to ruin my life and ministry. He could have destroyed both, but I was determined he was not going to succeed."

As a young bride Rexella dreamed of the day when she would have children. "Lots of little accordion players," she would say to Jack and her parents. But the day came when she had to admit that she might be a childless woman.

She claimed the verse in Deuteronomy 33:25 which promises ". . . as thy days, so shall thy strength be." But when the pain kept her in bed, Jack would kneel and pray for the pain to subside so she could sing in the evening. Rexella's family didn't even know what she was going through. A meaningful thought in Charles Spurgeon's devotional book, *Morning and Evening,* had captured her attention: "Wisdom hangs up the thermometer at the furnace mouth, and regulates the heat." She prayed for God's grace to see her through these painful times.

One of the strengths of Rexella is her quiet determination. And so she became accustomed to pain as a way of life; yet the joy of the Lord never left her during all those years of hoping.

"It is hard to be a childless woman when you have the heart of a mother," she told me as she fought to hold back the tears even after all these years.

Coping With Childlessness

Rexella underwent major surgery two times in order to improve the possibility of her having children, but the condition did not improve. "I identified with Hannah's weeping for a child. I couldn't understand the reason I was not allowed to have a baby."

In her distress, she cried out to God: "Lord, is it because I wouldn't be a good mother?"

She tried bargaining with the Lord, making promises to Him: "God, I'll keep on serving You; I'll keep traveling with Jack. I'll take the children with me."

But always she heard herself adding, "More than anything, I want Your will.

"In my flesh I didn't want to say it," she admits, "but with the help of the Lord I could pray, 'Thy will be done.' "

Her answer came in 1967. "I suffered a severe attack during a concert—an extreme case of endometriosis. I couldn't walk. My life was in danger. I needed a hysterectomy and I needed one now."

Rexella and her family have always been very close. Her older brother, Bob, led her to the Lord when she was sixteen. He was always a great source of spiritual blessing to her, and this crucial time in her life was no exception. He wisely said to her, "Rexella, you don't have to smoke to destroy the temple of the Holy Spirit."

She knew her brother was referring to her body in his gentle rebuke. She submitted to the surgery with her usual calm spirit.

God's "Something Better"

In the years preceding that decision and then following it, Rexella was often asked, "Why don't you have children? Don't you plan to have a family?".

An unthinking question, you may be feeling. Of course no one had any way of knowing, and Rexella handled it without bitterness. She had counseled many tearful women who confided to her *their* bitterness because they were childless and it was hurting their relationship with their husbands and with the Lord. Tenderly, she would hold them in her arms and cry with them, assuring them she understood how they felt.

Then she would take them aside and say, "There is only one thing better than having a family and that is having God's love. If you accept that and fill your life with His will—His purpose for you— then you can know satisfaction and fulfillment."

She shared with them how every time when she prayed about having a family, God would say to her in her inner spirit, *I have something better for you, Rexella.*

"I was never bitter, for which I give God the glory. I long for other women to know that God is not taking anything away from them or trying to hurt them. He *does* have something better. What could be better than children? Only having His will."

How Do You Handle Jealousy?

Many women have written or said to Rexella in person that they are jealous of the pregnant women they encounter, and the young mothers they see happily cuddling their babies.

"I know jealousy like that is hard to handle," she admits. "It is a natural feeling to want to be a mother. It is like having food taken away from you. How do you cope with hunger—hunger for children? You feel emaciated inside. At times you feel so empty and starved, and your emotions are so deep, it is hard to put into words.

"But even this can be overcome. It is through *knowing* God's purpose for your life and then *doing* it. It means totally trusting God."

Rexella found her comfort and help in the Bible. "God's Word to me has always been more than adequate. One of the things I had to learn early in our marriage was that I had to be submissive to God. In order to do that, I had to be willing to allow the Holy Spirit to help me as I read the Bible. As I came to understand His words to me, I drew strength and composure from them so that I could deal with the disappointments and heartaches.

"But in order for anyone to accept God's will, they first have to be convinced His will is best. Once I accepted that, I rejoiced in what my life with my husband could be. Jack and I came to realize that you don't have to have children in order to have a home and to be a family. Our home has been complete even though we have no children. Nevertheless, I am able to empathize with women who struggle with this and I always tell them it was the most difficult area in which God has dealt with me."

Rexella has enjoyed her nieces and nephews. And she urges women to seek other outlets for their maternal instincts—helping in the church nursery, teaching, or being a teacher's helper, foster parenting, and, of course, giving consideration to adoption.

Did she and Jack consider adoption? "Yes, but it was not God's will for us. We prayed this through and settled it long ago. A phone call came one night; someone offered us a child to adopt. It took a good deal of strength from the Lord to enable me to say no to that offer—in fact, it was the hardest thing I ever had to do. I cried. That is normal. Tears are God's tranquilizer. But I prayed for that child, that God would provide a mother to love and nurture that little one. I adopted that baby in my heart."

She didn't experience the peace in her heart that would have been the signal needed to go through with adoption. Because of their age, and their expanding ministry—which by then had become international in scope—Rexella and Jack felt this was the right decision and, instead, the Holy Spirit confirmed in her heart that she would be a mother to thousands of spiritual children won to Christ through their outreach. She emphasizes that she knows God makes no mistakes and He does have His way of letting us know what His will is in a given matter.

"Self-Taught" From the Word

Hers has certainly been an unconventional sort of life. She attributes her contentment to the many long hours she has been able to spend in quiet meditation. In the course of their travels, and with very little social life, she had more time than the average woman could possibly find to study and read the Bible.

"I discovered that if I really let the Holy Spirit get hold of me, the Word would speak to me."

If Rexella had started out as the wife of a traveling evangelist in the seventies or eighties, she might have walked into a Christian bookstore and come out with her arms loaded with books and tapes that could have provided quick insight. But back in the fifties and sixties such help was not as readily available.

"I just dug into the Bible and uncovered answers. I learned how to be a wife, how to dress, how to react to the temperaments of others. And, as I stored God's Word in my heart, I noticed the Holy Spirit coming to my rescue in a variety of circumstances, bringing verses to mind to help me act and react. I learned that if I would remind myself that God was in charge there could be victories and demonstrations of God's power that couldn't come in any other way."

In addition, she enhanced her education by observing pastors' wives. Most of them provided good examples; but some did not! The worst advice she ever received was from one woman who said, "Keep your husband humble; don't be afraid to keep sticking pins in him." Deflating Jack was not Rexella's idea of helping her husband. She became instead an encourager.

Rexella has never forgotten the good advice of an older man who took her aside and whispered, "Your husband has been a great blessing to me. Keep loving him. It will put iron in his spine."

She speaks warmly of the "love-level" of their relationship. "Monitor your love-level closely, for love is the very foundation of marriage. When love wanes, the foundation crumbles and you have nothing on which to build. If you have confidence in the love of the person with whom you walk, you can go through fire."

A Tide of Blessing

Standing-room-only crowds followed Jack and Rexella's ministry wherever they went. Ten million attended their citywide crusades in their last nine years of evangelistic meetings. There was a tide of blessing running and unusual results crowned their efforts. Jack's Scripture-packed messages reached people's hearts; churches were revived and helped. Rexella's dedication and love were communicated to the audiences and they, in turn, loved her for it and responded to the wooing of the Holy Spirit.

She always asked the Lord to make each crusade a new challenge and to keep her spirit fresh. When she looked out at the audience, she didn't see an ocean of indistinct faces, but individuals, specific people to whom she was drawn.

"I felt the Holy Spirit was guiding me to pray for these individuals —especially if they came several nights—and I developed a personal burden for them. Many times they responded to the invitation and I was able to walk down from the platform and go immediately to them." The audiences surged forward, eager for her tender touch and prayer, and the help and counsel Jack provided.

A Different Kind of Audience

In 1976, the Van Impes launched their nationwide television ministry through hour-long, prime-time specials, reaching a viewing audience estimated, at that time, as high as 30 million people three times a year. Then their weekly television program "Jack Van Impe Presents" made its debut on January 1, 1980.

This giant step, which immediately doubled their operating budget, required giant faith. But the response was overwhelming. Now they have a different kind of audience—one they cannot see, but letters and calls to the Van Impe headquarters in Royal Oak, Michigan, bear consistent witness to the impact the program is making. Because of the challenging problems in our society, Rexella has delved even more intently into the Scriptures, searching for the truths to convey to anxious hearts that will help to stabilize individuals as they walk through the inevitable conflicts that confront them on a weekly basis.

"I find I am confident in my interviews and discussions if I am knowledgeable about what God has to say," she relates. "The Word of God is relevant to everything we do and every issue we face in the world today."

But she also goes into her interviews thoroughly prepared. When talking, for instance, to David Biebel about his book, *Jonathan, You Left Too Soon*, describing the death of his three-year-old son and how they handled it, Rexella said, "David, when you looked to heaven, did you say, 'Lord, *why* my son?' "

Knowing the whys that all but consume us at such times in our life, Rexella was able to articulate the feelings and questions of her listeners. Her guest had responded by admitting to conflicting thoughts and feelings that swept over him at the time, and the anger with which he struggled. "I wrestled with this almost on a weekly basis. . . ." David Biebel is a pastor, and so it was encouraging to viewers to know that pastors hurt, cry, and question God, too. Rexella and her guest helped the viewing audience understand the grief process.

On another occasion, in interviewing Georgi Vins, who spent many years in a Russian concentration camp somewhere in Siberia, and learning of the death of Pastor Vins' father, Peter, who died because of his faith while in a prison camp, Rexella was observed struggling to hold back tears as she said, "It makes my heart so very sad."

But she had done her homework and asked thought-provoking questions that stimulated the thinking of viewers as they heard the dialogue between her and this man who had suffered at the hands of his communist tormentors.

The Van Impes attend the National Religious Broadcasters (NRB) convention held in Washington each January. Rexella has been a guest in the home of the vice president and his wife. On that occasion, she interviewed Barbara Bush and had an especially delightful experience visiting with her. Each year she makes it a point to seek out Christians in government and engages congressmen and senators in lively discussions, bringing these representatives of the people into listeners' living rooms.

In talking to Senator Bill Armstrong (from Colorado), Rexella asked, "Is there an improvement in the spiritual climate in Washington?"

The senator responded affirmatively, but then explained, "Some people feel that if you have a bunch of Christians in office it's going to correct all the problems. I don't feel that way. I think that what Christ said was not that we were going to have an easy time of it, but, in fact, great difficulty. But if we have men and women in Congress, and in the executive branch, and in the Pentagon, and in the county courthouses, and in the judiciary, and in television— wherever big decisions are being made—who see their vocation as being under the Lord, who pray for guidance in the conduct of their official responsibility, it's going to change the destiny of our country. Of course it's going to change the individual as well; but it's bound to have its effects."

On another occasion, as she interviewed Congressman Mark Siljander (from Michigan), Rexella stated, "I have the feeling, Congressman, that you feel Christians should be involved in politics."

Without hesitation, the congressman replied, "There's no doubt in my mind that Christians need to be praying for America. They need to be fasting on behalf of the country and interceding for the holocaust we're in with death technology—abortion and genetic engineering—as well as for other critical issues that face the nation. I believe that Christians, because of their faith and their praying, have, in fact, been given a reprieve of God's wrath on our country. But, by the same token, the Bible says that faith without works is dead! It says Nehemiah prayed, fasted, and interceded for Judah in the city—and the gates were burning and the walls were crumbling. But Nehemiah also went before the king and asked if he and his men could put their hands to work and rebuild the walls and the gates. That was practical work, and I believe Christians should do the same. So yes, in answer to your question, Rexella, Christians should be involved in politics."

Always the Tender Touch

Whether she is talking to a political figure, an author, a police chaplain, a college president, a well-known musician, a divorced woman left with eleven children to support, a single woman, a homemaker, or an interior designer—whomever—the possibilities are as endless as the interests and lives of people everywhere; viewers know they can expect a stimulating conversation.

Part of Rexella's tender touch is her beautiful singing voice. She has produced a total of eight music albums to date. And she writes a monthly column in their organization's newsmagazine.[2] The reality of God's love, power, and provision are clearly seen in her writing, singing, and television hostessing.

As you are turning the television knob and you come across an attractive, petite blond, as she incisively, but pleasantly interviews her guests, whatever the subject, it is a sure thing that they will be treated with a tender touch.

---

1. Rexella Van Impe, *The Tender Touch* (Nashville: Thomas Nelson Publishers, 1980).

2. *Perhaps Today*, published by Jack Van Impe Ministries, Box J., Royal Oak, MI 48068.